P9-BVG-732

THE GREENHAVEN PRESS
*Literary Companion*
TO BRITISH LITERATURE

READINGS ON

# GULLIVER'S TRAVELS

Gary Wiener, *Book Editor*

David L. Bender, *Publisher*
Bruno Leone, *Executive Editor*
Bonnie Szumski, *Series Editor*

Greenhaven Press, Inc., San Diego, CA

Every effort has been made to trace the owners of copy-
righted material. The articles in this volume may have
been edited for content, length, and/or reading level. The
titles have been changed to enhance the editorial purpose.
Those interested in locating the original source will find
the complete citation on the first page of each article.

Library of Congress Cataloging-in-Publication Data

Readings on Gulliver's travels / Gary Wiener, book editor.
    p.    cm. — (The Greenhaven Press literary
companion to British literature)
    Includes bibliographical references and index.
    ISBN 0-7377-0342-3 (lib. bdg. : alk. paper) —
ISBN 0-7377-0341-5 (pbk. : alk. paper)
    1. Swift, Jonathan, 1667–1745. Gulliver's travels.
2. Satire, English—History and criticism. 3. Voyages,
Imaginary. I. Wiener, Gary. II. Series.
PR3724.G8 R43  2000
823'.5—dc21

                                     99-047985

Copyright © 2000 by Greenhaven Press, Inc.
PO Box 289009
San Diego, CA 92198-9009
Printed in the U.S.A.

*"Expect no more from Man
than such an Animal is
capable of, and you will every
day find my Description of
Yahoes more resembling."*

—*Jonathan Swift,*
letter to the Reverend Thomas Sheridan

# CONTENTS

Foreword                                                    8

Introduction                                               10

Jonathan Swift: A Biography                                12

Characters and Plot                                        31

## Chapter 1: Background to *Gulliver's Travels*

### 1. An Introduction to Satire *by Leonard Feinberg*    41
*Gulliver's Travels* is one of the world's greatest satires. Unless
the reader understands the principles of satire, much of the
book's meaning may be lost. Satire, a necessary art, often
highlights mankind's follies and pokes fun at all that is
ridiculous in human affairs.

### 2. Swift's World *by Philip Pinkus*                    51
Jonathan Swift lived in a time of political upheaval, nearly
continuous warfare, and rapidly changing philosophies.
This tumultuous period produced some of the finest satire
ever written, including *Gulliver's Travels*.

### 3. The Enthusiastic Reception of *Gulliver's Travels*
*by A.L. Rowse*                                            57
Swift intended *Gulliver's Travels* as an indictment of humanity. He wrote more to trouble than to entertain his
readers. Nevertheless, his contemporary readership was
delighted with the book, and even to this day, *Gulliver's
Travels* survives as a story less noted for its savage satire
than for its ability to delight children and adults.

### 4. *Gulliver's Travels* and *Robinson Crusoe*
*by Nigel Dennis*                                          65
Jonathan Swift read voluminously in contemporary travel
literature before composing *Gulliver's Travels*. The most famous of such works, Daniel Defoe's *Robinson Crusoe*,
stands in complete opposition to Swift's notorious satire.
While Defoe celebrated man's ability to persevere and overcome all obstacles, Swift writes a biting satire on human
frailty.

5. **Swift's Satire of English Politics**
   *by Matthew Hodgart*     76
   While Swift's commentary on English politics in *Gulliver's Travels* had little effect on his contemporaries' thinking, the author knew that he was writing a book for the ages as well. The same follies and foibles Swift attacked in eighteenth century England have always been present among mankind.

## Chapter 2: Theme and Technique in *Gulliver's Travels*

1. **The Failure of Language in *Gulliver's Travels***
   *by Brian Tippet*     82
   In each new land that Gulliver visits, he must learn a new language, and the use of words emerges as a major theme in the novel. In each of these worlds, language is weakest when it is most complex and strongest when most simple.

2. **The Frailty of Human Beings in *Gulliver's Travels***
   *by Paul Fussell*     91
   As a product of the eighteenth century, *Gulliver's Travels* suggests the dual manner with which contemporary thinkers regarded mankind. While most humanists celebrated the accomplishments and abilities of humans, a contrary notion, implicit in the many physical ailments Gulliver is subjected to during his travels, implies that man's weaknesses are at least as prevalent as his strengths.

3. **Gulliver Is an Unreliable Narrator**
   *by Karen Lawrence, Betsy Seifter, and Lois Ratner*     96
   In the fashion of travel literature of his day, Gulliver meticulously reports every detail of his travels to far-off and mysterious lands. However, in adhering so fastidiously to minor points, Gulliver misses the larger implications of his travels.

4. **Swift's Technique of Reducing Men to Machines Enhances the Satire** *by John M. Bullitt*     100
   Swift often uses the technique of reducing intellectual concepts to mechanical, physical actions, as a way to mock humanity's lofty pretensions. Battles over wearing high or low heels, or breaking eggs at the big or small end lower, complicated human ideas to the level of physical comedy.

5. **_Gulliver's Travels_ Parodies First-Person Memoirs**
   *by J. Paul Hunter*     105
   While most commentators deny that *Gulliver's Travels* parodies other works of its time, Swift subtly pokes fun at Daniel Defoe's *Robinson Crusoe* and other eighteenth-century first-person narratives.

6. **Lagado: Swift's Satire of Scientific Knowledge**
   *by Clive T. Probyn*                                          110
   Through the mad schemes of the Projectors in the city of
   Lagado, Swift satirizes the proceedings of the English Royal
   Society, a group of scientists founded in 1660. Swift believes
   that issues of morality are more important than scientific
   knowledge.

# Chapter 3: Gulliver's Four Voyages

1. **Size as Metaphor in Lilliput** *by Jack G. Gilbert*          116
   In the first part of the *Travels*, Gulliver is as morally up-
   right as he is large. His magnanimity is contrasted with the
   treacherousness of the Lilliputians, who prove to be as
   small-minded as they are tiny.

2. **Size and Social Values in Brobdingnag**
   *by Howard Erskine-Hill*                                      123
   Just as readers start to admire Gulliver for his conduct in Lilliput, Swift reverses the situation. When Gulliver displays
   moral inferiority to his new hosts, readers are forced to
   abruptly reject him and wonder about their own ethics.

3. **Lilliput and Brobdingnag: Swift's Experiment
   in Optics** *by W.A. Speck*                                   134
   By shrinking and then magnifying human beings in Lilliput
   and Brobdingnag, Swift is able to draw humor as well as
   serious reflections on the nature of man. European society
   fares badly when compared with the Lilliputian or Brobdingnagian cultures.

4. **Hopeless Worlds: The Third Voyage**
   *by Michael DePorte*                                          141
   Swift wrote the third voyage of *Gulliver's Travels* last, after
   he had completed the section about the Houyhnhnms. Swift
   depicts reason run to extreme in the lands in Part III. But
   perfection is not a human quality, as Swift depicts through
   the harebrained schemes of the Projectors and the fearful
   eternal lives of the Struldbruggs.

5. **The Limitations of the Houyhnhnms**
   *by Boris Ford*                                               147
   Early commentators on Part IV of *Gulliver's Travels* viewed
   the Houyhnhnm society as a utopia based on logical thinking. The Houyhnhnm society is far from perfect, however,
   and the reader must realize that Swift the satirist is mock-
   ing the limitations of mankind, yet not suggesting that
   people can possibly live in the manner of the Houyhnhmns.

# Chapter 4: Reactions and Continuing Relevance

**1. In Defense of Jonathan Swift**
*by William Hazlitt*                                        155

*Gulliver's Travels* presents a sobering view of human beings. Swift's brilliance was in his character. If he was inwardly a bitter, angry man, this harsh temperament produced the insightful wit and biting satire of his writings.

**2. *Gulliver's Travels* Is the Product of a Sick Mind**
*by William Makepeace Thackeray*                           160

Such a depraved vision of mankind could only come from within the man himself. Swift must be rebuked for his shameful, blasphemous production.

**3. Swift's Unhappy Utopia** *by George Orwell*            166

Jonathan Swift was an unhappy man who could see no possibility of joy in this world and had no belief in an afterlife. His utopian vision in *Gulliver's Travels* is therefore manifested in the dull, coldly rational world of the Houyhnhnms. Despite its limitations, *Gulliver's Travels* remains a great work of art that contains many unpleasant truths about the human condition.

**4. Reading *Gulliver's Travels* as a Child and as an Adult** *by Marcus Cunliffe*                       174

Adults who return to *Gulliver's Travels* years later after having read it as a child find the book to be a very different experience. Swift's writings have been dismissed as the ravings of a diseased mind, but there is much truth to be found in his "inconsistent" masterpiece.

Chronology                                                 181

For Further Research                                       184

Index                                                      186

# FOREWORD

*"'Tis the good reader that
makes the good book."*

Ralph Waldo Emerson

The story's bare facts are simple: The captain, an old and scarred seafarer, walks with a peg leg made of whale ivory. He relentlessly drives his crew to hunt the world's oceans for the great white whale that crippled him. After a long search, the ship encounters the whale and a fierce battle ensues. Finally the captain drives his harpoon into the whale, but the harpoon line catches the captain about the neck and drags him to his death.

A simple story, a straightforward plot—yet, since the 1851 publication of Herman Melville's *Moby-Dick*, readers and critics have found many meanings in the struggle between Captain Ahab and the whale. To some, the novel is a cautionary tale that depicts how Ahab's obsession with revenge leads to his insanity and death. Others believe that the whale represents the unknowable secrets of the universe and that Ahab is a tragic hero who dares to challenge fate by attempting to discover this knowledge. Perhaps Melville intended Ahab as a criticism of Americans' tendency to become involved in well-intentioned but irrational causes. Or did Melville model Ahab after himself, letting his fictional character express his anger at what he perceived as a cruel and distant god?

Although literary critics disagree over the meaning of *Moby-Dick*, readers do not need to choose one particular interpretation in order to gain an understanding of Melville's novel. Instead, by examining various analyses, they can gain

8

numerous insights into the issues that lie under the surface of the basic plot. Studying the writings of literary critics can also aid readers in making their own assessments of *Moby-Dick* and other literary works and in developing analytical thinking skills.

The Greenhaven Literary Companion Series was created with these goals in mind. Designed for young adults, this unique anthology series provides an engaging and comprehensive introduction to literary analysis and criticism. The essays included in the Literary Companion Series are chosen for their accessibility to a young adult audience and are expertly edited in consideration of both the reading and comprehension levels of this audience. In addition, each essay is introduced by a concise summation that presents the contributing writer's main themes and insights. Every anthology in the Literary Companion Series contains a varied selection of critical essays that cover a wide time span and express diverse views. Wherever possible, primary sources are represented through excerpts from authors' notebooks, letters, and journals and through contemporary criticism.

Each title in the Literary Companion Series pays careful consideration to the historical context of the particular author or literary work. In-depth biographies and detailed chronologies reveal important aspects of authors' lives and emphasize the historical events and social milieu that influenced their writings. To facilitate further research, every anthology includes primary and secondary source bibliographies of articles and/or books selected for their suitability for young adults. These engaging features make the Greenhaven Literary Companion series ideal for introducing students to literary analysis in the classroom or as a library resource for young adults researching the world's great authors and literature.

Exceptional in its focus on young adults, the Greenhaven Literary Companion Series strives to present literary criticism in a compelling and accessible format. Every title in the series is intended to spark readers' interest in leading American and world authors, to help them broaden their understanding of literature, and to encourage them to formulate their own analyses of the literary works that they read. It is the editors' hope that young adult readers will find these anthologies to be true companions in their study of literature.

# INTRODUCTION

*Gulliver's Travels* endures. Whether as a children's book, an animated cartoon, a satiric novel, a full-length motion picture starring Ted Danson and Mary Steenburgen, or even in spirit as a search engine on the Internet named when two Stanford graduate students consulted a dictionary and selected the word *yahoo* for their company moniker, *Gulliver's Travels* refuses to die. In addition to *yahoo*, the book has added *Lilliputian* and *Brobdingnagian* to the dictionary and given new meaning to the term *horse sense*.

One measure of *Gulliver's Travels'* greatness is that it can be read on so many levels. Many readers are children when they first meet Gulliver, just as they are when they meet Huck in *The Adventures of Huckleberry Finn*, or Alice in *Alice in Wonderland*. There is a certain charm, an innocence, in the story of a man towering above a six-inch civilization and an equal interest—as the popular *Honey, I Shrunk the Kids* and its sequels suggest—in suddenly finding oneself in a society where all things—even rats and the moles on human faces—are ten times normal size.

Ironically, Swift was not writing for children. In the narrowest of terms, he was constructing a political satire in which many of his characters were based on the movers and shakers of late eighteenth- and early nineteenth-century England. Swift wished to skewer many of his political enemies as well as those critics who found fault with the ordained priest's beloved Anglican Church. His political attacks were a dangerous practice in a society where freedom of speech was not protected, but Swift the satirist never backed down before his enemies.

*Gulliver's Travels* is also, quite obviously, a travel book. Or rather, it is a satire of travel literature, a hoax concocted by Swift and made to seem realistic by the introductory letter, the maps, and the publisher's note that accompany the actual text. Swift even used the name of Lemuel Gulliver as the book's writer, not himself, so that many in his reading audience wondered about the identity of this new English author, or tried to locate Lilliput or Brobdingnag on a real map.

*Gulliver's Travels* is also a comic novel in which much of the humor is decidedly *not* for children. Instances of adult humor are evident from the novel's opening pages, where Swift, who wrote the book only a handful of years after Daniel Defoe's *Robinson Crusoe,* manipulates the name of Gulliver's master, Mr. Bates. The careful reader realizes that Swift is commenting on why the dissenting Protestant, Defoe, never mentions anything about Crusoe's sexuality during the lengthy time that the man was stranded on his island. In Lilliput, Gulliver's ingenious but scandalous method of dousing the fire in the empress's chambers is quintessential Swiftian scatological humor. And when the tiny Gulliver views the court ladies in Brobdingnag from a far-too-intimate perspective, his reaction is anything but prurient.

Above all, *Gulliver's Travels* is a book about how we live our lives; or rather, it is about how we s*hould* live our lives, if, as Swift sees it, we humans were really rational animals instead of animals *capable* of reason. Swift claimed in a letter, contrary to much public and critical opinion, that he was not a misanthrope in the ordinary sense of hating all humans. He loved individuals, he declared, but hated mass man and the evil and folly perpetrated by groups of humans. "I hate and detest that animal called man, although I heartily love John, Peter, Thomas and so forth," he wrote. Like any good satirist, Swift hoped that his writings might open some eyes. "I have finished my Travels," he wrote a friend in August 1725, "They are admirable Things, and will wonderfully mend the World." Perhaps Swift wanted to believe this, but given his typically ironic wit, one can imagine that there is more cynicism and doubt than wishful thinking in the remark.

Ultimately, in the words of Edmund Gosse, in his *History of English Literature:* "Whether we read it, as children do, for the story or as historians, for the political allusions, or as men of the world, for the satire and philosophy, we have to acknowledge that it is one of the wonderful and unique books of the world's literature."

Such sentiments led George Orwell to include *Gulliver's Travels* among the six books he would save if all others were to be destroyed. Despite our contemporary, technological world—or perhaps because of it—*Gulliver's Travels* will endure for a long time to come.

# JONATHAN SWIFT: A BIOGRAPHY

It may surprise readers to learn that Jonathan Swift, who
wrote one of the most famous travel books of all time, never
traveled beyond the British Isles. While he was often on the
move during his lifetime, particularly in journeying between
Ireland and London, Swift never visited the European conti-
nent, and he never embarked on any long sea voyages of the
type so carefully described in *Gulliver's Travels*. The man
who dreamed up Lilliput, Brobdingnag, Laputa, and
Houyhnhnms Land was a world traveler only in his imagination, where he charted previously undiscovered fictional
territory. A fiercely independent, freethinking man, Swift
clearly marched to the beat of a different drummer. As his
early biographer, Lord Orrery, said of Swift, "You must never
look upon him as a traveler in the common road."

Swift was a man of many careers: poet, political emissary
and propagandist, religious leader, and, of course, literary
satirist. One might think that *Gulliver's Travels* would be the
central focus of any biography of Swift, but his career was so
rich that most biographers spend little time on Swift's masterpiece, choosing to concentrate on this towering figure's
numerous other accomplishments. Nevertheless, in addition
to *Gulliver's Travels*, Swift also wrote what is arguably the
single most famous essay in Western civilization, the brilliantly satirical "A Modest Proposal," published in 1729.

Swift the author is also a towering figure in the history of
English and Irish writing, of satire, and of travel fiction. In
particular, the rich history of Irish literature—which in-
cludes novelist James Joyce; playwrights John Millington
Synge, Samuel Beckett, and Brendan Behan; and poet W.B.
Yeats, some of the more highly regarded writers on the
planet—must begin with the man known simply as "the
Dean," Jonathan Swift. The renowned American science-
fiction writer Isaac Asimov puts the case for Swift plainly:
"The greatest of the English satirists, by common consent, is

Jonathan Swift." Yeats, himself among the most celebrated of twentieth-century poets, acknowledged the Dean's power: "Swift haunts me," Yeats wrote. "He is always just round the next corner." And T.S. Eliot, also on the short list of the greatest twentieth-century poets, extended such praise to the man as well as to the writing when he called Swift "the greatest writer of English prose, and the greatest man who has ever written great English prose."

## EARLY LIFE AND EDUCATION

Almost nothing was normal in the life of Jonathan Swift. As with other prominent figures who lived centuries ago, we have facts, or perhaps assumptions, but details may be sketchy and explanations rare. From the beginning, Swift's life reads like a cheap romance novel. The second child of English parents, he was born on November 30, 1667, at 7 Hoey's Court in Dublin, Ireland. His father, Jonathan, after whom the writer is named, had died eight months before, leaving his widow, Abigail (née Erick), both financially and emotionally unable to support her family. Nevertheless, young Jonathan had a nurse, retained through the goodness of his uncle Godwin Swift, a wealthy businessman and lawyer.

Despite such humble beginnings, there loomed an auspicious background that would forever affect Swift's life and career. He was related, on his father's side, to one of England's greatest poets, John Dryden, and, more importantly, his uncle Godwin had a close friendship with Sir John Temple, a powerful political figure of the era. Swift would later use this allegiance to gain employment with Temple's son, Sir William, and his service in the Temple household would prove to influence him in every possible way, from his political philosophy to his personal friendships.

The central event of Swift's earliest years is so odd that it might almost be disbelieved if we didn't have it in Swift's own words. In this autobiographical fragment, which Swift wrote in the third person, he describes the event:

> When he was a year old, an event happened to him that seems very unusual; for his nurse, who was a woman of Whitehaven, being under an absolute necessity of seeing one of her relations, who was then extremely sick, and from whom she expected a legacy, and being at the same time extremely fond of the infant, she stole him on shipboard unknown to his mother and uncle, and carried him with her to Whitehaven, where he continued for almost three years. For, when the matter was

discovered, his mother sent orders by all means not to hazard a second voyage, till he could be better able to bear it. The nurse was so careful of him, that before he returned he had learnt to spell; and by the time that he was three years old he could read any chapter in the Bible.

This early journey was the first of numerous trips that Swift would make back and forth across the Irish Sea during his lifetime. When his nurse finally did return five-year-old Jonathan to Dublin, his mother was gone. She herself had now left for Leicester, England, to live with a relative. She remained in Leicester for the rest of her life. Swift was raised by the family of his uncle Godwin, who took care of his physical needs as well as his education. But something was missing emotionally. One early biographer, W.E.H. Lecky, writes,

> Swift was on affectionate terms with many members of his family, but of his Uncle Godwin he always spoke with bitterness. He considered him hard, penurious, and grudging in his favours, and he even accused him of having given him the "education of a dog."

As Lecky notes, the truth of these matters is hard to ascertain, for Swift received "the best education Ireland could afford." Subsequent biographers have doubted that Swift ever made the remark, but it has persisted as one of the legendary stories about the Dean.

Jonathan's uncle sent the six-year-old to the Kilkenny Grammar School, located sixty miles southwest of Dublin, where he remained for eight years. There is little available information about Swift's stay at Kilkenny. Biographer A.L. Rouse writes,

> He received the usual education of a public school [meaning private school in Great Britain] of the time, strictly based on the classics, but particularly Latin. Swift became fairly widely familiar with Latin literature, though not very proficient at verse-making, the *fine fleur* [best part; cream] of a classical education.

Swift's study of Latin had a profound influence on his later philosophy of literature. A conservative in aesthetics as well as in his politics, he upheld the classical Roman and Greek authors, whom he preferred to the more contemporary British authors.

In 1682, when Swift was fifteen, he enrolled at Trinity College in Dublin. But he was not apparently satisfied. As the son of English parents, Swift always considered himself English, not Irish. This paradox would reach a peak in later years when he would be celebrated as an Irish hero despite his assertion that "I am not of this vile country, I am an Englishman." Swift would have preferred to attend a more prestigious English school such as Oxford, but, as would be the case for almost all the rest of his life, he would have to be content in an Irish setting.

Swift proved an indifferent student at Trinity. He spent more time reading poetry and history than studying for his classes in Latin, Greek, and Aristotelian philosophy. Swift blamed his rebelliousness on the inattention of his uncle Godwin. "By the ill-treatment of [Swift's] nearest relations, he was so discouraged and sunk in his spirits that he too much neglected his academic studies," Swift wrote in his autobiographical fragment. He was continually in trouble throughout these years. He rebelled against the college's rules and was disciplined on numerous occasions, often for failing to attend mandatory religious services. Swift's contrary conduct ultimately resulted in the harshest penalty of all: in 1686 he received his degree *speciali gratia,* a designation intended to suggest that he had not really earned his diploma but was receiving one anyway through the school's good graces. Swift nevertheless stayed on at the college in pursuit of a master's degree, and he continued his wayward conduct. In March 1687 he was disciplined for neglecting his duties and carousing in town. In November 1688 he was forced to beg for forgiveness on one knee after having insulted the junior dean.

Despite these setbacks, some good came of Swift's years at Trinity. He was already engaged in writing satires—spoofs and parodies—including the initial draft of the work that would eventually become *A Tale of a Tub.* In his classes, the preferred method of teaching was through a formal system of debates. Students would argue the pros and cons of a given proposition. Among the themes for dispute was this one:

Man is a rational animal.

No horse is rational.

Only rational animals are capable of discipline.

Biographer David Nokes points out that despite Swift's mediocre grades at Trinity, "As *Gulliver's Travels* demonstrates, Swift was clearly paying attention when these themes were debated."

## BRITISH HISTORY AND SWIFT

Jonathan Swift's personal history is wedded to the social, political, and religious history of the British Isles. The era was one of great political upheaval in England as various religious factions and political parties fought for control of the state. In *Gulliver's Travels*, after hearing Gulliver's account of English affairs, the king of Brobdingnag not inaccurately describes England's last century as "an heap of conspiracies, rebellions, murders, massacres, revolutions, banishments, the very worst effects that avarice, faction, hypocrisy, perfidiousness, cruelty, rage, madness, hatred, envy, lust, malice, and ambition could produce."

Swift was descended from conservative supporters of the king and the Anglican Church (the Church of England). In 1649 King Charles I was beheaded for alleged crimes against the state, and for eleven years England was ruled by Protestant dissenters led by Oliver Cromwell, who felt that the Church of England was too closely aligned with Catholicism. This era, often referred to as the interregnum period (between kings), ended when Charles's son, Charles II, was restored to the throne in 1660, seven years before Swift was born.

Charles II died in 1685, and James II, his brother and successor, who had converted to Catholicism some years before, ascended the throne. In 1688 James was forced from the throne, and the Protestants William and Mary were installed as English monarchs. The deposed James II fled to Ireland hoping to gain sympathy from its Catholic majority, raise an army, and regain the English throne. In Ireland, this turmoil was referred to simply as "the Troubles." Swift was forced to abandon his quest for a master's degree when many of his teachers fled to England. He decided to take the opportunity to visit England himself and see his mother in Leicester.

### THE INFLUENCE OF SIR WILLIAM TEMPLE

During this stay with his mother and her relatives, Swift used his family connection to the Temples to gain employment with Sir William Temple, first at Sheen, on the river Thames west of London, and later at Moor Park in Surrey, southeast of London. Sir William, who was the same age as Swift's uncle Godwin, was retired from English political life and spent his time writing, philosophizing, and gardening. He had served England as a diplomat and numbered among his accomplishments the forging of "the Triple Alliance" of Sweden, England, and Holland designed to thwart French king Louis XIV's territorial ambitions. He was also instrumental in arranging the marriage of William and Mary.

The exact nature of Swift's initial employment is still debated by biographers, but it is clear that the stay with Temple had a lifelong affect on the young man's thinking and writing. So sketchy are the facts of Swift's relationship to Temple that some historians argue that Swift was actually his employer's illegitimate son. But there is no solid evidence to sustain this conjecture. The common belief is that Swift served as his new patron's secretary, and that Temple, who was writing his memoirs and various essays, found the intelligent young man useful in this capacity. Swift also tutored Esther Johnson, who was fourteen years younger than he and the daughter of a servant in the household. Swift, who all his life was fond of wordplay, nicknamed Esther "Stella," by which he would refer to her for the rest of their lives.

Sir William was a Whig, one of the two dominant parties in English politics. Whigs supported the revolution of 1688 and the monarchy of William and Mary. They tended to uphold the middle class and favor mercantile interests. In matters of religion, Whigs were more understanding of Protestant dissenters and were stridently anti-Catholic. Tories, on the other hand, represented the old landed aristocracy and believed in the divine right of kings. Thus, many Tories, who were called Jacobites, supported the monarchy of the deposed James II. Swift found himself siding with Temple in such political matters, but his allegiance would shift within a matter of years.

In 1689 Swift had the first attack of giddiness, nausea, and headaches that would plague him throughout his life. We now understand the cause to be Ménière's disease, a disorder of the inner ear characterized by abnormal sensation of movement (vertigo), loss of hearing in one or both ears, and noises or ringing in the ear. To this day there is no cure for Ménière's disease, but the symptoms may be treated with a wide range of pharmaceuticals. In Swift's day, however, nothing was known about his illness, and Swift alternately blamed his diet or the English air. In 1690 he returned to Dublin, hoping the change of atmosphere would restore his health, but the trip was in vain. He returned to Moor Park in October 1691.

While working for Temple, Swift's literary career began in earnest. He published his first poem, "Ode to the Athenian Society," in 1691. This poem, and Swift's other odes of the period, were heavily influenced by Temple's style and beliefs. Legend has it that when Swift showed this poem to one of his relatives, the famous English poet John Dryden, the great writer told him, "Cousin Swift, you will never be a poet."

Not all went well during Swift's first stay with the Temples. Early on, he felt as if he were treated with coldness and distrust. His self-confidence, perhaps overconfidence, alienated those in the family who felt that a young man as poor as Swift ought not to be so presumptuous. But he slowly gained Sir William's confidence as the older man was forced to acknowledge the young man's substantial gifts.

In July 1692 Swift left Temple to pursue a master's degree from Oxford, the premier university in England. After completing his degree, Swift returned to the Temple household, where Sir William found him increasingly useful. But Swift wished for more, and he found the quiet, isolated atmosphere of Moor Park frustrating. He longed to set out on a career of his own and hoped that Sir William's political power would aid him in this resolve. Temple, apparently reluctant to part with the valuable young man, tried to placate Swift by sending him on diplomatic errands. On one occasion Swift appeared before King William III to present Sir William's proposal for holding elections every three years, a proposal that the king rejected.

But even this "treat" was not enough for the ambitious Swift. In May 1694 he left the Temple household once again, resolved to enter the Anglican Church as a priest. Though he would serve the church for the remainder of his life, most biographers believe that Swift was not particularly religious and that the church offered him his only means to get ahead in a world where his various patrons, beginning with Sir William, for one reason or another failed to help Swift rise in the secular world. On October 25, 1694, Swift was ordained a deacon in the (Anglican) Church of Ireland, and in early 1695 he was appointed to a position as vicar of Kilroot, near Belfast, in northern Ireland. But he was very soon dissatisfied with his duties in this isolated and nonreligious town, and by May 1695 he had left his position and returned to Moor Park. Before leaving, he proposed marriage to a young woman, Jane Waring, who, in his usual manner, he had nicknamed "Varina." Waring, however, turned him down.

## THE BATTLE OF THE BOOKS AND A TALE OF A TUB

Again Swift fell under the influence of Sir William's literary philosophy. As a conservative, Temple preferred classical writers of ancient Rome and Greece to those of the seventeenth century. But Temple was not a particularly thorough scholar and wrote a piece in support of the *Epistles of Phaliris*, which he believed to have been written in ancient times. Temple was embarrassed when other scholars, led by Richard Bentley, proved that the epistles were fake. But Swift rose to Temple's defense by writing *The Battle of the Books*, a work that satirizes Temple's antagonists by portraying debate as a mock-heroic, or comic, battle for literary supremacy between ancient and modern books. The book would be published in 1704, along with another book that Swift completed during this period, *A Tale of a Tub*.

Regarded by scholars as a witty, inventive masterpiece (some even believe it to be Swift's finest work), *A Tale of a Tub* is an allegory of the religious situation in Swift's contemporary Britain. *A Tale* tells the story of three brothers—Peter, Martin, and Jack—who function as personifications of the Catholic, Anglican, and dissenting churches, respectively. Their adventures symbolize the history of religion in Great Britain, with Martin, representative of Swift's own Anglican beliefs, getting much the better treatment throughout. But *A Tale* is such an idiosyncratic work that it cannot be adequately summarized: Swift's satiric pen is unleashed upon religion, learning, extremism, readers, and even the writing of books. As with many of his works, Swift did not claim authorship but instead credited the book to a persona, a literary hack, whom he could then use to discredit modern writing. *A Tale of a Tub* bears the satiric subtitle *Written for the Universal Improvement of Mankind* and claims that the "truly Learned" reader will find enough profound information within it "to employ his Speculations for the rest of his Life." One chapter in this quirky work is entitled "A Digression in Praise of Digressions." Elsewhere, toward the end of the work, Swift's hack writes, "I am now trying an Experiment very frequent among Modern Authors; which is, to write upon Nothing; When the Subject is utterly exhausted, to let the Pen still move on."

## SWIFT'S FINAL YEARS AT MOOR PARK

Swift used his return to Moor Park to reacquaint himself with his former protégé, Esther "Stella" Johnson, who was now a teenager. Their relationship blossomed into a lifelong friendship. Swift would help Stella with her reading and writing, and she aided him in his secretarial duties. As biographer Victoria Glendinning writes, "He and she created a world of their own, bent over their books and papers, by means of a private, allusive baby-language; Swift was verbally ingenious and agile. He had a great liking for codes, riddles and puns."

Of Stella's personal qualities that so attracted him, Swift would later write,

> I knew her from six years old, and had some share in her ed-
> ucation by directing what books she should read, and perpet-
> ually instructing her in the principles of honour and virtue
> from which she never swerved in any one action or moment
> of her life. She was sickly from her childhood until about the
> age of fifteen, but then grew into perfect health, and was
> looked upon as one of the most beautiful, graceful, and agree-
> able young women in London, only a little too fat. Her hair
> was blacker than a raven, and every feature of her face in per-
> fection. . . . Never was any of her sex born with better gifts of
> the mind, or who more improved them by reading and con-
> versation.

Swift's last stay with the Temples is often regarded as the quietest and happiest four years of his life. As an ordained priest, he was more highly regarded in the Temple house-hold. He was now in his late twenties, a fully mature man, and Temple came to rely on his abilities more than ever. Nevertheless, there were disappointments. Temple had lured Swift back to Moor Park with the implied promise of a church position in England, an appointment that never ma-terialized. Upon Sir William's death in January 1699, Swift inherited one hundred pounds and, in Swift's words, "the care, and trust, and advantage of publishing his [Temple's] posthumous writings." But even this position as Temple's lit-erary executor would prove troublesome. Temple's memoirs contained sensitive material that was offensive to some in high society. Martha Giffard, Sir William's sister, did not want the book published until those who stood to be of-fended, including Giffard's friend Lady Essex, were de-ceased. But Swift went ahead and published the memoirs in 1709, ten years after Temple's death. As biographer Glendin-ning says, "The repercussions of his decision . . . was one among many contributions to his failure to land 'the great fish' of ecclesiastical preferment in England which he so much wanted and always expected."

## BACK TO IRELAND

Indeed, Swift's career was one of continual disappointment. As the son of English parents, he always considered himself an Englishman. As such, he tended to share the general English prejudice against the Irish, and he dearly wanted an appointment in England, not Ireland. Swift was convinced that Sir William's influence with King William would land him a church position in prestigious Canterbury or Westminster. As Swift explains in his autobiographical fragment, upon the death of Sir William,

> Mr. Swift removed to London, and applied by petition to King William upon the claim his Majesty had made to Sir William Temple. . . . Col. Henry Sidney, lately created Earl of Romney, who professed much friendship for him, and was now in some credit at Court . . . promised to second Mr. Swift's petition, but said not a word to the King. And Mr. Swift, having totally relied on this lord's honor, and having neglected to use any other instrument of reminding his Majesty of the promise made to Sir William Temple, after long attendance in vain, thought it better to comply with an invitation, given him by the Earl of Berkeley, to attend him to Ireland, as his chaplain and private secretary.

But even this modest appointment was not to be Swift's. According to Swift's account, another man, Arthur Bushe, "insinuated" his way into Berkeley's favor and was awarded the secretarial position.

But Swift's situation improved. In February 1700 he was given a position as vicar of Laracor, northwest of Dublin, and in October of the same year he was awarded a prebend, or honorary position, at St. Patrick's Cathedral in Dublin. In February 1701 Swift completed the doctor of divinity degree at the University of Dublin. From this point on he would often be referred to as Dr. Swift.

In 1701 Esther Johnson, who had inherited land in Ireland from Sir William Temple, crossed over the Irish Sea with her companion, Rebecca Dingley. They would provide much companionship for Swift in the ensuing years. Nevertheless, the lure of England remained great for Swift. Between 1701 and 1714 he would make numerous journeys between Dublin and London and become increasingly involved in English politics.

It was also during this period that Swift began publishing his work in earnest. In 1701 he anonymously published a treatise, *Dissensions in Athens and Rome*, about liberty and tyranny. When *A Tale of a Tub, The Battle of the Books*, and *The Mechanical Operation of the Spirit* were released together in 1704, the book quickly sold out four editions. Though Swift published the volume anonymously, those in literary circles quickly ascertained its author, and Swift's reputation as one of the new bright lights on the British literary scene was secured. His work quickly captured the attention not only of the public but also of various major literary voices of the time—among them Joseph Addison, Richard Steele, and John Arbuthnot—with whom Swift would later become close friends.

Among Swift's literary triumphs was a clever satire of astrology published as "Predictions for the Year 1708" by one Isaac Bickerstaff. The ever-rational Swift especially despised the false science of astrology, whose leading Irish practitioner at the time was John Partridge. Partridge had been printing almanacs containing astrological predictions and had challenged his readers to try their hand at predictions to see if they might do any better. In his satirical "Predictions," Swift went so far as to declare that Partridge would die of a fever on a certain night. Then, in 1709, Swift gave such a convincing account of Partridge's final days that readers believed the astrologer was indeed dead. Even when Partridge produced his next almanac and asserted that he was alive, readers did not believe him. As biographer David Nokes writes, "The Bickerstaff hoax was a stunning example to Swift of the manipulative powers of the press. What had begun as a simple practical joke grew into a full-blown fantasy until more people knew of Partridge's death than had ever heard of him alive." Soon afterward, Swift would turn his journalistic genius toward more important political situations.

## LONDON POLITICS

In 1706 Dublin's superior archbishop sent Swift to London as an emissary to present a case for the abolition of the "first fruits" tax on Irish clergymen. As the Church of England was exempt from such a fee paid to the Crown, so Swift argued that the Irish church should be accorded a similar exemption. During the course of several trips to London in the years that followed to pursue his case against the first fruits tax, Swift, still a Whig, was introduced to two important Tories, Robert Harley (the earl of Oxford) and Henry St. John (Viscount Bolingbroke). The two men quickly recognized Swift's abilities, and it was not long before he was writing in support of Tory causes. As Victoria Glendinning writes, "What [they] wanted from him was his pen and his wit and his talent. Dr. Swift became their spin-doctor, writing propaganda for [their] policies, satirizing the opposition, testing opinion." Between November 1710 and June 1711, Swift wrote *The*

*Examiner*, a weekly Tory paper consisting of a single unsigned article.

Swift's change of allegiance was not without reason. The Whigs had been less than forthcoming with Swift as he negotiated for the removal of the first fruits tax; they also seemed willing to make concessions to the dissenters, which troubled the Anglican Swift. And, as we shall see, they were also pro-war: Any reader of *Gulliver's Travels* knows that Swift was an ardent opponent of militarism.

Both William and Mary had died by 1702, and the new monarch was Queen Anne. Much of the political satire in *Gulliver's Travels* stems from Swift's observations as a political player during the late years of Queen Anne's reign and the early years of her successor, George I, who assumed the throne upon her death in 1714. During Anne's reign, England was immersed in the War of the Spanish Succession, led by John Churchill, the duke of Marlborough. The ruling Whigs supported this war, designed to continue British supremacy against upstart France and Spain, but the Tories favored peace. In 1711 Swift brought forth a pamphlet, "The Conduct of the Allies." In this pamphlet and several that followed, Swift attacked the duke of Marlborough and attempted to influence the public against the war. Four editions of "The Conduct of the Allies" were needed to satisfy the public's craving for Swift's brilliantly reasoned argument. The Whigs denounced the work, and some urged that Swift be impeached. But that same year the Tories rose to power in Parliament, and negotiating secretly, they brought about the Treaty of Utrecht in 1713.

The next year, 1714, saw the death of Queen Anne and a Whig rise to political supremacy. Oxford, Bolingbroke, and their like were out, and George I and the Whig administration of Robert Walpole were in. Swift would never again occupy such a privileged position in English politics.

## THE LITERARY LIFE

Swift made many friends in the literary community during his stay in London. Among these were some of the era's greatest writers. Though his switch to the Tory cause alienated Whigs such as former friends and accomplished writers Richard Steele and Joseph Addison, Swift now found himself getting to know the poet Alexander Pope, whose literary triumphs include "The Rape of the Lock," "An Essay on Man," and a translation of Homer; John Gay, celebrated author of

*The Beggar's Opera;* and John Arbuthnot, writer and personal physician to Queen Anne. Along with Lord Oxford and another writer, Thomas Parnell, the group formed the Scriblerus Club in 1713 and planned a collaborative book, the fictional biography of the writer Martin Scriblerus, which was to be a broad satire on modern folly. Though the biography was never published, Swift's writings with the Scriblerus Club contained the seeds of what would become *Gulliver's Travels.*

During his stay in London, Swift kept in touch almost daily with "the ladies," as he called them, Stella and her companion, Rebecca Dingley, who remained in Ireland. His writings give a lively and candid account of his years at the forefront of English political life. These letters, which fill a substantial volume, were later collected as *The Journal to Stella.* In these writings Swift mentions his visits to a Mrs. Vanhomrigh (pronounced "Van hummery") and her daughter Hesther, whom he nicknamed "Vanessa." He had met the Vanhomrighs years before, and they had formed his London family in much the same way as "the ladies" were his Irish support group. Vanessa would become the second important woman in Swift's life—in fact, she fell madly in love with him, a situation that would make Swift highly uncomfortable, especially in light of his "friendship" with Stella. Vanessa would write to him, "I was born with violent passions, which terminate all in one—that inexpressible passion I have for you."

## THE DEAN

Just before the fall of the Tories, Swift's patron, Lord Oxford, had obtained for him the position of dean of St. Patrick's Cathedral in Dublin. As usual, Swift had hoped for more. He believed that his proven worth to the Tories would set him up with at least a bishopric in the Church of England, but once again, with his satiric writings and partisan politics, Swift had made enough enemies in high places to ensure that he would have to be content with a position in the country of his birth, Ireland, and not the England of his ancestry. In a letter to Stella, he described his feelings: "At my first coming I thought I should have died with discontent, and was horribly melancholy while they were installing me, but it begins to wear off and change to dulness."

But soon Swift became accustomed to his new position in Dublin. Victoria Glendinning describes Swift's life as dean:

Swift was a conscientious and authoritarian dean, involving himself deeply in every detail of the cathedral's ritual and routine: the quality of the music . . . , the training of the choir, the quality of the preaching, the demeanour of his clergymen when "outside." He revived what was then considered the primitive practice of consecrating, administering and himself receiving the Sacrament of Holy Communion on Sunday. He was jealous of his authority, challenging [his superior] Archbishop King on appointments and preferments over which they both had influence, and testing his own privileges, and his rights of decision and veto . . . to their legal limits. It took him about six years to get his empire under control.

Swift also sought to get his private life in order. He moved Stella and Rebecca Dingley to Dublin to be near him, and together with other new friends, they formed his family. Swift's relationship with Stella is a point of contention among biographers. For propriety's sake, Swift was wary of having her always by his side and claimed that he was never alone with her at any time. Nevertheless, there are biographers who claim that, in 1716, Swift and Stella were secretly married. Absent of proof, this scenario seems unlikely, but nothing can be completely dismissed in the life of the very unordinary dean of St. Patrick's.

Meanwhile, Hesther Vanhomrigh had not given up on Swift. Their friendship continued, as Swift occasionally visited the love-stricken woman. He made his relationship with her the subject of his celebrated poem, "Cadenus and Vanessa," (*Cadenus* is an anagram of *decanus,* Latin for "dean.") The poem was not published until 1726, the same year as *Gulliver's Travels* appeared, and three years after Vanessa's death. Like Stella, Vanessa too had moved to Ireland to be near Swift. She was quite aware of her rival, and in 1720 her jealousy finally bubbled over: She wrote to Stella to inquire about the exact nature of her relationship with the Dean. Swift was furious, and he let Vanessa know it. It is said that Vanessa died of a broken heart, but logic has it that she succumbed in 1723 to the same tuberculosis that had taken her sister.

Having been ousted from English politics, a man of Swift's talents and wide-ranging interests could not help but enter into those of Ireland. Almost despite himself, Swift, who had once written, "I reckon no man is thoroughly miserable unless he be condemned to live in Ireland," became an Irish hero. In 1720 his anger at the English treatment of the Irish resulted in *A Proposal for the Universal Use of Irish Manu-*

*factures, &c.*, which urged that the Irish reject English goods. But it was his publication of *The Drapier's Letters* in 1724 that gained him enormous popularity.

The subject of *The Drapier's Letters* was Wood's halfpence, a cheap copper coin with which the English planned to flood the Irish market, greatly profiting the mother country and devaluing Irish currency. Posing as a *drapier*, or linen draper, Swift wrote his letters against this plan and raised such a cry among the public that the scheme was abandoned. English authorities attempted to learn the identity of the author and pursue prosecution, but although many in Ireland knew of Swift's role, none betrayed Ireland's new savior. As for Swift, he denied any special interest in Irish causes, crediting his interference more to his strong beliefs about right versus wrong. "What I did for this country," he said, "was from profound hatred of tyranny and oppression. I believe the people of Lapland or the Hottentots cannot be so miserable a people as we."

## GULLIVER'S TRAVELS

The idea for *Gulliver's Travels* had been germinating in Swift's mind since his Scriblerus days. Travel writings were popular reading, and Swift immersed himself in books of the genre. In particular, he read the *Voyages* of William Dampier, a seaman and pirate who could list, among his many remarkable adventures, the rescue of Alexander Selkirk, the man on whom Daniel Defoe's *Robinson Crusoe* (1719) would be based.

From Swift's letters, we know that by 1721 he was hard at work on *Gulliver's Travels*. He wrote to his friend Charles Ford, "I am now writing a history of my Travels, which will be a large volume, and gives account of countries hitherto unknown; but they go on slowly for want of health and humor." Swift's health improved. He wrote the first two voyages in 1721–1722, and the fourth, to the land of the Houyhnhnms, was completed by January 1724. The voyages to Laputa and other lands that were to make up Part Three were actually written last. Swift interrupted *Gulliver's Travels* at this point to write *The Drapier's Letters*, and he finished the book in 1725. In August 1725 he wrote, "I have finished my Travels and I am now transcribing them. They are admirable things, and will wonderfully mend the world."

Swift poured his entire life and times into *Gulliver's Travels*. Easily identifiable in the text are all of the abuses of government, religious quarrels, political intrigues, scientific excesses, sexual ambiguities, and other human follies that Swift himself experienced or witnessed firsthand. Originally intended as a direct satire on the Whigs, the book grew into much more. Swift's target ultimately included the whole of human stupidity, and from Swift's point of view, there was an awful lot of human stupidity.

In 1726 Swift journeyed to London carrying the manuscript of what would become his masterpiece. As was his modus operandi, Swift had *Gulliver* printed anonymously bearing the title, *Travels into Several Remote Nations of the World*. The suppression of Swift's name was a wise choice. With its barely disguised political satire, the book, he believed, would likely get him into at least as much trouble as had his previous attacks on public figures. There was another reason for anonymity, however. As in the cases of Isaac Bickerstaff and the drapier, Swift wanted Gulliver to come to life so that *Gulliver's Travels* would seem as real to its readers as the nonfictional travelogues, such as Dampier's, that were so popular in eighteenth-century Europe. Swift even went so far as to make the fictional Gulliver a cousin of Dampier in the letter from Gulliver to Richard Sympson that serves as a preface to the book.

Upon its publication in November 1726, the book was an immediate success. Swift was not in London to experience the reaction firsthand, having left for Dublin when he learned that Stella was ill. His friend John Gay summed up the general reaction in a letter to the Dean:

> About ten days ago a Book was publish'd here of the Travels of one Gulliver, which hath been the conversation of the whole town ever since: The whole impression sold in a week; and nothing is more diverting than to hear the different opinions people give of it, though all agree in liking it extremely. 'Tis generally said that you are the Author, but I am told, the Bookseller declares he knows not from what hand it came. From the highest to the lowest it is universally read, from the Cabinet-council to the Nursery.

Swift's major disappointment was that the publisher, Benjamin Motte, toned down some of the satire and even inserted less-offensive passages. One could hardly blame him, however, because eighteenth-century printers were often arrested for the crimes of their authors, especially anonymous ones. In a letter to Charles Ford, Swift complained about these unauthorized changes: "The whole Sting is taken out in several passages, in order to soften them. Thus the Style is debased, the humor is quite lost, and the matter insipid." It was not until the 1735 Faulkner edition of *Gulliver's Travels* that Swift's book was printed as he originally intended.

Meanwhile, Swift's decision to publish *Gulliver* anonymously was having its intended effect. The hoax was on. As John Arbuthnot wrote to Swift:

> Gulliver is in every body's Hands. Lord Scarborow who is no inventor of Storys told me that he fell in company with a Master of a ship, who told him that he was very well acquainted with Gulliver, but that the printer had Mistaken, that he lived in Wapping, & not in Rotherhith. I lent the Book to an old Gentleman, who went immediately to his Map to search for Lilly putt.

Swift wrote to Alexander Pope from Dublin to say that "a Bishop here said, that Book was full of improbable lies, and for his part, he hardly believed a word of it."

## ILLNESS, DEATH, AND PREDICTED DEATH

By March 1727 Stella had recovered from her illness, and Swift was once again off to London to visit with old friends, including Pope and Bolingbroke. But it was not a pleasant visit. While staying at Pope's home in Twickenham, Swift's Ménière's disease resurfaced with a vengeance, and he was plagued by deafness and vertigo. Then came the news that Stella was ill again and very near dying. Swift was racked with despair. "I have been long weary," he wrote, "of the world, and shall, for my small remainder of years, be weary of life, having for ever lost that conversation which could alone make it tolerable." He returned to Dublin and would never visit England again. Stella died on January 28, 1728.

Stella's death threw the already morose Swift into a despondency from which he would never quite recover. These emotions would be heightened by the losses of other friends, among them Gay in 1732, Arbuthnot in 1735, and Pope in 1744. In 1731, thirteen years before his own death, Swift composed the witty and poignant poem "Verses on the Death of Dr. Swift." In it, Swift imagines his friends discussing his myriad infirmities:

> See, how the Dean begins to break:
> Poor Gentleman, he droops apace,
> You plainly find it in his Face:
> That old Vertigo in his Head,
> Will never leave him, till he's dead:
> Besides, his Memory decays,
> He recollects not what he says;

> He cannot call his Friends to Mind;
> Forgets the Place where last he dined.

Toward the poem's end Swift ably defends his satire, the "sting" of his writings at which so many took offense:

> Perhaps I may allow, the Dean
> Had too much Satyr in his Vein;
> And seem'd determin'd not to starve it,
> Because no Age could more deserve it.
> Yet, Malice never was his Aim;
> He lash'd the Vice, but spar'd the Name.
> No Individual could resent,
> Where Thousands equally were meant.

## FINAL YEARS

Swift's last years have always been an enigma, partly because early biographers were so keen to equate the writings with the man. What is clear is that for many years the loss of his friends and the increased severity of his Ménière's disease and other infirmities induced a state of melancholy that dominated his life. His often quoted letter to his cousin Martha Whiteway, who served as his companion in these late years, gives a sense of the magnitude of his depression:

> I have been very miserable all night, and today extremely deaf and full of pain. I am so stupid and confounded, that I cannot express the mortification I am under both in body and mind. All I can say is, that I am not in torture; but I daily and hourly expect it. Pray let me know how your health is, and your family. I hardly understand one word I write. I am sure my days will be very few; few and miserable they must be.

This letter, his last, was written five years before his death. "Good night, I hope I shall never see you again," was the valediction he reportedly said to his friends at the end of a typical evening. In 1742 a Commission in Lunacy formally declared Swift to be of unsound mind and memory. For many years after, especially in the staid Victorian era of the nineteenth century, biographers attempted to suggest that Swift's mental decline was evident even in *Gulliver's Travels*, where the misanthropy of the fourth voyage was so wide-ranging and pervasive that the book could only be the product of a madman. This view has been thoroughly discredited by modern scholars. "The failure of Swift's faculties towards the end of his life, some fifteen or sixteen years *after* the publication of *Gulliver's Travels*, has been seized upon to explain something the critics neither liked nor understood," writes critic Louis A. Landa. "It seemed to them valid to push his 'insanity' back in time, to look retrospectively at the intolera-

ble Fourth Voyage of *Gulliver*, and to infer that he must have
been at least incipiently mad when he wrote it." Modern biographers now understand Swift's state late in his life as the
natural progression of old age and senility rather than of
mental illness. As biographer Irwin Ehrenpreis has written,
"Swift was no more neurotic than [Alexander] Pope or [Dr.
Samuel] Johnson. The tradition of his madness has been rejected . . . by every qualified scholar who has bothered to look
into the question."

Swift died on October 19, 1745, at the age of seventy-seven.
In his will, with a typically Swiftian satiric gesture, he left a
large sum of money to establish a hospital for the mentally
ill. He had explained the reasons for this as far back as 1731,
in his "Verses on the Death of Dr. Swift":

> He gave the little Wealth he had,
> To build a House for Fools and Mad:
> And shew'd by one satyric Touch,
> No Nation wanted [needed] it so much.

Swift was buried in St. Patrick's Cathedral in Dublin, not
far from his companion Stella. The poet W.B. Yeats asserted
that Swift sleeps under the greatest epitaph in history. Written by Swift in Latin, it may be translated as follows: "Here
lies the body of Jonathan Swift, Doctor of Divinity, dean of
this Cathedral Church, where savage indignation can no
longer lacerate his heart. Go traveler, and imitate if you can
one who with all his might championed human liberty."

# CHARACTERS AND PLOT

*Emperor of Lilliput:* The emperor is twenty-eight years old, over six inches tall, and has reigned for seven years. He is known far and wide as "the Delight and Terror of the Universe." He initially likes Gulliver and grants him his freedom, but several in his court who are Gulliver's enemies insist that he put Gulliver to death. He settles for a compromise by which Gulliver will be blinded and eventually starved to death, thus demonstrating the emperor's great mercy.

*Flimnap:* The treasurer of Lilliput, he despises Gulliver because of the immense cost of feeding and maintaining "the Man-Mountain." Flimnap comes to believe the ludicrous idea that his wife and Gulliver are seeing each other in an inappropriate manner.

*Glumdalclitch:* Gulliver's "Little Nurse" is nine years old and forty feet high ("being little for her age.") She is the daughter of the farmer who first discovers him in Brobdingnag. She continues to look after Gulliver even after he is bought by the queen.

*Gulliver:* Trained as a surgeon, Gulliver goes to sea when his medical practice fails. He is an honest, ethical gentleman who can be clever and resourceful. But he is also somewhat naive and simplistic about the ways of the world. His restlessness and curiosity propel him to seek adventure. After living with the Houyhnhnms, he develops a great hatred for mankind and sleeps in the barn among his horses.

*The Houyhnhnms:* This breed of horselike characters is civilized and lives entirely by the principles of reason. The Houyhnhnms have a very limited language, which has no words for vices such as lying, cheating, and stealing because these concepts do not exist for them.

*King of Brobdingnag:* A wise and thoughtful ruler, the king governs fairly, by applying common sense and reason. He questions Gulliver on the ways of Europe and finds Europeans to be "little odious vermin." The king is a man of high morals; he rejects Gulliver's offer to teach the Brobdingnagians how to make gunpowder.

*Lord Munodi:* A former governor of Lagado, Munodi has been deposed for being too practical. He has a beautiful mansion in the country but worries that he must tear it down and build a new, dilapidated version based on modern principles. Munodi is said to represent Oxford and/or Bolingbroke, Swift's two deposed Tory patrons.

*Pedro de Mendez:* A generous Portuguese sea captain, de Mendez offers to transport Gulliver back to England for no monetary recompense. He is kind, generous, and thoughtful, a marked contrast to the Yahoos with whom Gulliver has been comparing mankind.

*Reldresal:* The Lilliputian secretary, Reldresal is also Gulliver's friend. During the impeachment hearings, he argues for a more lenient punishment than death—putting out Gulliver's eyes.

*Skyresh Bolgolam:* The *glabet*, or high admiral of Lilliput, he is Gulliver's mortal enemy from the start. When Gulliver captures the fleet of Blefescu, Bolgolam's hatred increases, as his own military prowess is diminished by this great victory. Bolgolam favors putting Gulliver to death for alleged crimes against the state.

*The Struldbruggs:* This small group of people in Luggnagg live forever. But instead of a blessing, eternal life is a curse. Although these Struldbruggs never die, they continue to age. Thus, after the age of eighty, they live the remainder of their lives in senility and bodily decrepitude.

*The Yahoos:* Something of a cross between man and ape, these beasts display every negative quality imaginable. They smell atrociously, eat raw flesh, and fornicate wantonly. The Yahoos are virtually incapable of domestication.

## PLOT SUMMARY: PART I

*Gulliver's Travels* is the story of Lemuel Gulliver's four voyages into remote nations of the world. Gulliver, born in Nottinghamshire in central England, is trained as a surgeon. When his medical practice fails, he signs on as a ship's surgeon and makes several voyages. On May 4, 1699, Gulliver sets sail aboard the *Antelope*. A fierce storm arises, the ship is wrecked, and Gulliver finds himself alone, swimming toward shore. Exhausted, he feels he can swim no more when suddenly he touches bottom. He falls asleep on the shore.

When Gulliver awakens he cannot move. He has been tied

to the ground by thousands of minuscule ropes. He feels the sting of hundreds of tiny arrows and decides against trying to escape. Gulliver realizes that he has been captured by men no more than six inches tall who speak in a foreign tongue that he cannot understand.

Gulliver is transported to the capital city of Mildendo where he is imprisoned in an ancient temple yet treated well. The people call him Quinbus Flestrin, or "the Great Man-Mountain." The emperor orders his people, the Lilliputians, to provide him with food and teach him their language. Gradually Gulliver's docile nature impresses the emperor, and after signing a pledge of allegiance, Gulliver is given his freedom. Despite this, he has unaccountably made enemies in the court, particularly the high admiral, Skyresh Bolgolam.

Gulliver slowly learns about this tiny kingdom. There are two political parties, the high heels and the low heels, named after the height of their shoes, and two religious factions, the Big-Endians and Little-Endians, named for the side of the egg they crack open. The present king and political administration are Small-Endians; many Big-Endians have been exiled across the water to a neighboring enemy country, Blefescu.

As a condition of gaining his freedom, Gulliver pledges to help defeat the great fleet of ships in the harbor at Blefescu, which are preparing to attack Lilliput. Gulliver wades into the channel separating the two islands, and, warding off the arrows of the enemy troops (he saves his eyes by donning spectacles), he hauls nearly the entire fleet of Blefescu back to Lilliput. The emperor immediately declares him a Nardac, the highest honor he can bestow. But Gulliver loses favor when he refuses to complete the destruction of Blefescu and subject its people to the power of the Lilliputian emperor. Instead, he helps negotiate a peace that is quite favorable to Blefescu.

Gulliver soon provides what he thinks is another great service by dousing a fire that has broken out in the empress's chamber. However, he does so by urinating on the flames, and thus invokes the wrath of the empress and others in the court. Soon after, he is secretly informed that he is to be impeached for his crimes. His chief antagonists, Skyresh Bolgolam the high admiral and Flimnap the treasurer, argue that he should be put to death. But Reldresal, Gulliver's friend in the government, argues for a lesser punishment, that of blinding. A compromise is struck: Gulliver will first be blinded, then slowly starved to death.

Having already gained the emperor's permission to visit Blefescu, Gulliver leaves abruptly before the Lilliputians can enact their sinister plan. He had resided in Lilliput for nine months and thirteen days.

Gulliver is received warmly in Blefescu. One day, while walking along the shore, he spies an abandoned boat. Homesick for England, Gulliver persuades the emperor of Blefescu to provide hundreds of workers to help him make the vessel seaworthy. He sails off early on the morning of September 24, 1701. He is rescued by an English ship and taken home, where he shows off the tiny sheep and cattle he had transported in his pockets from Lilliput.

## PART II

Within two months of his return, Gulliver is once again ready to see the world. He signs on with a merchant ship called the *Adventure*. After a great and sustained wind blows the ship well off course, the crew stops for water on an unknown shore. Gulliver sees the other sailors frantically running for the ship, pursued by a gigantic creature. He alone is left behind. Struggling to make his way through a field of forty-foot grain, Gulliver is discovered by a farmer, who brings him home. There, he is cared for by the farmer's nine-year-old daughter, whom he names Glumdalclitch ("Little Nurse"). She cares for him, treating him like a pet, and teaches him her language.

Brobdingnag is an expansive country measuring six thousand miles long and up to five thousand miles wide. The people are proportionally as tall as the Lilliputians were tiny, averaging nearly sixty feet in height. Their features are huge and flawed, as grotesque as the Lilliputians' features were fair and unblemished. Gulliver decides that it is all a matter of proportion.

The farmer knows a cash cow when he sees one. Soon, Gulliver is performing before the townsfolk for money. Next, he is taken to the capital city of Lorbrulgrud. When Gulliver becomes ill from the strain of performing again and again, the farmer increases his schedule to make the most money he can before Gulliver dies. Fortunately, the queen is taken with the tiny man and buys him from the farmer. At Gulliver's request, Glumdalclitch is allowed to stay at the court to look after him.

Two boxes are designed for Gulliver as living quarters. One is a traveling box with a ring at the top for carrying.

Gulliver quickly becomes a court favorite. But he suffers many unenviable "adventures." Envy provokes the formerly smallest member of the court, a thirty-foot dwarf, to play some nasty tricks on the vulnerable Gulliver. On various occasions he drops Gulliver into a large bowl of cream, wedges him into a marrow bone, and shakes the branch of an apple tree so that the barrel-sized fruit come crashing down around Gulliver. Gulliver is also at the mercy of numerous other giant creatures. He is fetched by a spaniel, attacked by flies and wasps the size of birds, pelted by tennis-ball sized hail, and force-fed by a gargantuan monkey.

Gulliver is subjected to numerous other indignities. The court maids of honor think nothing of undressing before him, exposing their mottled skin and giant moles sprouting hairs thicker than packthread. Their perfume is overpowering enough to make him faint. Once, while walking in the countryside, Gulliver attempts to show his athleticism by leaping over a pile of cow dung. Unfortunately, he jumps short.

The king of Brobdingnag, a thoughtful and wise leader, spends five sessions with Gulliver learning about England and Europe and asking penetrating questions. Proud of his native land, Gulliver tells of its ways, including its political intrigues, rebellions, wars, massacres, revolutions, and conspiracies. When the sessions are finished, the king tells Gulliver that he finds "the bulk of your natives to be the most pernicious race of little odious vermin that nature ever suffered to crawl upon the surface of the earth."

Gulliver explains the power of gunpowder and offers to do the king a great service by teaching his workmen how to make it. But the king recoils in horror at the destructive power of this substance and commands Gulliver never to mention it again. Though Gulliver believes that this attitude will surely lessen an English reader's opinion of the king, it is clear that the Brobdingnagian leader's morals are as high as his size. He is that rare monarch who governs by "common sense and reason."

After two years in Brobdingnag, Gulliver journeys with the king and queen to the palace of Flanflasnic, on the south coast of the kingdom about eighteen English miles from the sea. One day, an eagle scoops up Gulliver's traveling box and carries him far out to sea, finally dropping him into the water. Once again Gulliver is rescued by an English ship and returned to his native land.

## PART III

Captain William Robinson, a friend of Gulliver's, persuades him to once again embark on a voyage, this time to the East Indies, with promises of increased pay and another surgeon to work under him. The ship sets sail on August 5, 1706, and, after surviving a fierce storm, it is boarded by pirates. When Gulliver complains to the buccaneers about their treatment of his crew, he is set adrift alone in a small boat with a modest supply of food.

Gulliver soon lands at the island of Balnibarbi near Japan, a colony of the flying island known as Laputa. He is hauled up to the flying island, which is steered by use of a large magnet, or lodestone, deep in its core. Laputa is ruled by a king and inhabited by philosophers who have but two interests: science and music. The men of Laputa are so engrossed in theoretical science that they ignore the practical. Their clothing is ill fitting and their houses lopsided. They cannot hold a conversation without the help of servants bearing "bladders" on sticks, who shake the stone-filled sacks in their ears when they are to listen and before their mouths when they should speak.

The king of Laputa maintains control over his colonies below by flying the island overhead if the colonists rebel. He can blot out the sun, causing famine and disease, or, in rare cases, lower the island to crush everything below. But during one such rebellion, three years before Gulliver's arrival, the people of Lindalino constructed large magnetized towers that threatened to pull the flying island to the ground permanently. By this scheme, the Lindalino people gained concessions from the king.

Gulliver quickly grows bored on the flying island because its men are interested only in science and music and, therefore, not in him. He gains permission to leave, visiting Lord Munodi, a former governor of Lagado, whose interest in ancient and practical measures has gained him nothing but scorn from the progressive government. In this crazy country, only Lord Munodi (believed by scholars to be modeled on Swift's Tory patrons Bolingbroke and Oxford), represents everything that is "magnificent, regular, and polite." His country house is a masterpiece of ancient architecture but designates him as an outcast. Munodi worries that he will be forced to modernize his home to avoid the king's displeasure.

Gulliver next visits the Grand Academy of Lagado, where

"projectors" engage in modern scientific study. In this satire on modern science, Gulliver finds projectors conducting various ludicrous experiments. One attempts to extract sunbeams from cucumbers; another tries to convert human excrement back to its original food; a third builds houses from the roof down; yet another breeds naked sheep. There are at least five hundred of these projectors at the Grand Academy, all engaged in projects of dubious usefulness.

Gulliver next visits Glubdubdrib, where he is politely received by the governor. Various forms of black magic are practiced here, and Gulliver is allowed to speak with many of the great figures of history, whom the governor calls up from the dead. In conversing with such luminaries as Alexander the Great, Julius Caesar, and Hannibal, Gulliver learns that accounts of these great men's lives are often completely inaccurate. History amounts to a pack of lies. Gulliver further learns that most often the good and worthy men in human history meet foul endings, but "bawds, whores, pimps, parasites, and buffoons" often triumph.

Upon visiting Luggnagg, Gulliver is excited at the prospects of meeting the Struldbruggs, a small group of immortals. Gulliver extols what must be their virtues, making a long speech about the benefits of living forever, and how worthy to lead and dispense wisdom these people must be. But he is soon corrected, for although the Struldbruggs have the gift of eternal life, they do not possess eternal youth. Instead, they age horribly, lapsing into senility and decrepitude. When he finally does see some of these immortals, Gulliver completely loses his appetite for eternal life. "No tyrant could invent a death into which I would not run with pleasure from such a life," he says.

Though the ruler of Luggnagg has taken a liking to Gulliver and offers him a position in his court, the homesick traveler wishes to return to his family. On May 6, 1709, Gulliver leaves Luggnagg, sailing for home by way of Japan and Holland. He arrives in England in April 1710.

## PART IV

Gulliver sets out on his final journey on September 7, 1710, as captain of the *Adventure*, a merchant ship of 350 tons. When various members of his crew die on the voyage, Gulliver is forced to replace them with a motley collection of criminals, who soon mutiny and lock Gulliver in his cabin. After several weeks, they maroon Gulliver on an unknown shore.

The first natives Gulliver comes across are the Yahoos, a bestial version of mankind covered with thick hair and having strong claws on their hands and feet. Gulliver remarks that "upon the whole, I never beheld in all my travels so disagreeable an animal, or one against which I naturally conceived so strong an antipathy." The Yahoos attack Gulliver, who holds them off with his sword; they spew him with their excrement until a horse nears and they run off. Another horse arrives, and the two seem to whinny a conversation. Gulliver follows one of the horses, a grey steed, home to its dwelling, a long building made of timber with a straw roof.

He soon realizes that the horses, called Houyhnhnms, are rational and can communicate. Gulliver, who soon learns their whinnying language, spends much of his time trying to convince the bewildered Houyhnhnms that he is not a Yahoo. Because they have no word for lying in their completely rational society, they wonder if, in telling his wild tales of Europe, Gulliver is saying "the thing which is not." During the course of Gulliver's three-year stay in Houyhnhnms Land, he comes to believe that Europeans are indeed Yahoos, and though he tries to distinguish himself from both the local and European Yahoos, he ultimately realizes that "I could no longer deny that I was a real yahoo in every limb and feature."

Gulliver is enraptured by the Houyhnhnms' society, which is based on reasonableness. Houyhnhnms engage in no disputes, as there is no partisanship, and reason always prevails. Evil is unknown. Houyhnhnms are decent and civil to each other, but have no need for ceremony. They have no pride regarding their meritorious conduct; there is no need to celebrate what they inherently are. Houyhnhnms always aid those in need, have no use for material things, and love all in their race equally. Gulliver is so taken with them that he begins to adopt their mannerisms and speech patterns and vows to live among these rational creatures forever.

But one day the Houyhnhnms' council meets and decides that a Yahoo, however impressive a Yahoo, should not be living among them. He is given two months to construct a canoe and leave Houyhnhnms Land. Devastated, Gulliver submits to this command. He sails to nearby New Holland, where he is attacked by savages and suffers an arrow wound to his knee. Finally he is rescued, against his will, and boards a Portuguese ship captained by the gentle and courteous Pedro de Mendez.

Gulliver arrives back in England on December 5, 1715. As he concludes his narrative, he informs the reader that it has been five years since his return to England, but he cannot stomach the thought of living among Yahoos or even with his wife and children, whose smell is vile to him. He still acts and whinnies like a horse, and he lives in the stable behind his house among two young horses with whom he converses at least four hours a day. He has begun to permit his wife and children to dine with him (at the other end of a long table), but fears he may never reconcile with English Yahoos. In particular, human pride is so offensive to him, he asserts, that anyone harboring this vice should never presume to appear in his sight.

# CHAPTER 1

# Background to *Gulliver's Travels*

READINGS ON
GULLIVER'S TRAVELS

e of the pleasures involved in the satiric experience,
re many, many others. One of the reasons why we
leasure from satire than from a sermon, even when
is making exactly the same point as the sermon, is
ve an uncomfortable feeling that the minister ex-
do something about it. We enjoy the satire because
that nobody really expects us to do anything about
we have no real intention of ever doing anything
may not be a moral reaction, but for most human
s the reaction.

poet] John Dryden preferred Juvenal to Horace
e former gave him more pleasure, although Horace
more instruction. "Pleasure, though but the second
is the first in favor. And who would not choose to be
r, rather than to be more esteemed?" Dryden was
appeal of satiric literature lies in the pleasure it
eader. It is not read for moral instruction. It is not a
for a sermon and is certainly not approached in the
tting a lesson in ethics. Satire may criticize evil but
ic elements are incidental, not primary. The essen-
is entertainment. Satire must please the reader by
ve richness as in *Gulliver's Travels* and *Brave New*
by vigor of invective as in Juvenal and [French
belais, or by sustained mockery as in [French writer]
*Candide*. Satire may offer other gratifications, but
sure it must give in order to hold the reader. That
may come from the incongruity of Swift's Lil-
or [French writer] Anatole France's penguins, or the
s in [comic strips] "Li'l Abner" and "Peanuts." It may
n an avoidance of the censor, as in [Swift's essay] *A*
oposal and *Jurgen,* or in jokes about bosses and of-
in the retorts of [comedian] Groucho Marx. It may
the pleasure in recognizing the contrast between
d the pretended, as the social satires of Voltaire and
novelist] Sinclair Lewis and [British playwright]
haw reveal that contrast.

eal of satire lies in its literary merit: brilliance, wit,
shness. But its longevity depends on the material to
se techniques have been applied. Because we have
itioned by our society, we usually do not find en-
that which seriously opposes what we have come to
socially appropriate behavior. The satire that sur-
material that continues to be significant, and issues

# An Introduction to Satire

Leonard Feinberg

Unless the reader understands that *Gulliver's Travels*
is a satire, much of the book's point may be lost.
Leonard Feinberg provides an overview of the genre
of satire, stressing its strengths and weaknesses, and
defending satire against those who suggest that it is
an inferior form. Feinberg believes that satire, however unfair it is toward its target, is a necessary art,
one that is based more in artistic pleasure than in
morality. Feinberg ultimately defines satire as "a
playfully critical distortion of the familiar." Leonard
Feinberg has taught at Iowa State University. He is
the author of *The Secret of Humor* and *Introduction
to Satire*, from which this selection is taken.

Like other arts, the best satire is concerned with the nature of
reality. Unlike other arts, which emphasize what *is* real, satire
emphasizes what *seems* to be real but is not. It ridicules man's
naive acceptance of individuals and institutions at face value.
That ridicule may be expressed in amused or in bitter terms,
but the essence of satire is revelation of the contrast between
reality and pretense. [French writer] La Rochefoucauld says,
"We all have sufficient strength to bear up under the misfor-
tunes of others."

Like the fable and allegory, satire almost always pretends
to be something other than what it really is. (Sometimes it
succeeds so well that readers miss the satiric intention entirely, as children do reading *Gulliver's Travels*.) But unlike
the fable and allegory, satire does not always teach a moral
lesson or offer a desirable alternative to the condition it criticizes. Readers sometimes assume that the satirist is offering a
positive solution, in the form of behavior which is exactly opposite to that displayed in his satire, but this rarely proves to

be true when one gets to know the satirist. And even direct satire, in the form of expository prose, is a pose: the satirist pretends to be giving objective, factual information but actually he is exaggerating and distorting facts.

Although satire often contains both humor and criticism, attempts to find the precise amount of each are not particularly useful. In Juvenalian satire [modeled after the work of the Roman poet Juvenal] there is likely to be a minimum of humor, and in Horatian satire [modeled after the work of the Roman poet Horace] a minimum of criticism. But though in theory the humor can be separated from the criticism, in practice comic devices are constantly used in order to criticize. Perhaps the best way to determine, in each case, whether humor or satire is being used is to evaluate the intention. "The laughter of comedy is relatively purposeless," David Worcester suggests. "The laughter of satire is directed toward an end.". . .

## SATIRE USES DISTORTION

It is generally assumed that satire appeals primarily to the intellect. But the mechanism of satire is not that simple. The intellect seeks order. But the basic technique of satire is distortion, usually in the form of exaggeration, understatement, and pretense; and distortion implies disorder. A popular satiric method of achieving distortion is incongruity, which also results in disorder. Reason, then, is used to create unreason; logic is used to create illogic. [The German philosopher] Schopenhauer called humor an escape from "the tyranny of reason," yet humor is an appeal *to* reason. [Literary critic Henri] Bergson was so convinced that satire (and all other humor) should appeal only to the intellect that he required for its presence "an anesthesia of the heart." But most of the great satirists are anti-intellectual, distrustful of logically reached generalizations, and skeptical about the validity of all dogmas concerning men and institutions. "The only way to get rid of a temptation," says [Irish playwright] Oscar Wilde, "is to yield to it."

There are several reasons why satirists distrust theory. For one thing, being inconsistent human beings themselves, they are painfully aware of the contradictions between logic and fact. For another, most satirists suspect that people choose a philosophy and an ethic not to redirect their lives to nobler ends, but to justify the kind of life they are already leading. Also, satirists know that almost all absolute generalizations

about men and institutions ar
there are exceptions to the rule,
ization, contradictions to the
Schopenhauer's story of the n
about man being made in God's
walked by.

## PLEASURES OF SATIRE

Satire offers the reader the plea
release of aggressions. Both of t
derision, and some defenders of
gentlemanly a quality could be
scholar, for example, insists that
is not derision but a noble "n
Bredvold's gesture is well meant
derision and man enjoys derisio
at himself. There is nothing cy
nothing harmful to satire. Anyo
writing could be spoiled by ack
spirit will not be mollified by a s
dignation. And no one honest er
lighted by vigorous ridicule need
his pleasure. Most people find
satirists have made the most of
Heinrich Heine said of [French w
vanity is one of his four Achilles'

The excesses that we laugh at a
the fat man, not the strong ma
greed, not philanthropy. Literatu
tack has always been more po
praise and agreement, and Para
pealed to more readers than P
satirist, attack is likely to result i
ing; defense and praise are likely
are justified. But this aggression
can be expressed in the form of v
sembled anger is an unpleasant
about.

We read satire because it give
disagree about the *kind* of pleas
suggest that the pleasure is a mo
a "good" reader with a "good" sa
dignant at a miscarriage of justi

that remain relevant, long after the time when the satire was written.

## SATIRE AND MORALITY

The assumption that satire relies on moral norms is so widely accepted that one hesitates to challenge it. But moral norms are not easy to define. Many satirists consider their work moral even when it contradicts the satire of other writers who also call themselves moralists. The same milieu produced the bohemian satire of Oscar Wilde, the socialist satire of Bernard Shaw, and the Catholic satire of Gilbert Chesterton; the conflicting satires of Dryden, Andrew Marvell, and Lord Rochester; Samuel Johnson and Charles Churchill; Roy Campbell and W.H. Auden. If moral norms, were, the criteria, readers would not enjoy satire based on the amoral or immoral norms of [such satirists as] H.L. Mencken, Norman Douglas, Luigi Pirandello, Samuel Beckett, William Wycherley, James Joyce, Wilde, Bernard Mandeville, Machiavelli, and Jean Genêt.

Before accepting the morality theory, we might ask: *Whose* moral norms is satire based on? A universal norm? It is hard to prove that one exists, except in such vague terms that even bitterly opposing satirists claim simultaneously that they adhere to it. A democratic norm? There has also been satire on behalf of communism, fascism, and aristocracy. A Christian norm? Satire appears, in every society, including atheistic Russia and skeptical China. Some readers approve only of didactic satire [which teaches a lesson], Thomist [after the teachings of St. Thomas Aquinas] or humanist [concerned with human beings] or Marxist [after the teachings of Karl Marx]. But others, quite as well informed, prefer destructive satire which provides what Robert Brustein calls a "purely purgative function, relieving the spectator of his outrage and frustration."

## APPLYING SOCIAL NORMS

Of course satire relies on norms. The moment one criticizes and says that something has been done in the wrong way, he is implying that there is a right way to do it. The "right" way has been interpreted by some to mean the moral way, but that is only one of the possible criteria. In actual practice, satirists usually apply a standard not of morality but of appropriateness—in other words, a *social* norm. It is a norm concerned not with ethics but with customs, not, with morals but with mores; and it may be accepted by an entire society, or only one class in that society, or just a small coterie. The more exclusive the norm, the less likely the satire is to have wide appeal. Still, works complying with specialized tastes do provide satire for audiences which share those tastes. . . .

It is also true that what is called "great" satire, satire which achieves lasting acceptance, is likely to depend on norms that seem to be universal, values that transcend their own time and locale. In that sense social norms tend to overlap with widely accepted moral norms; from that gray area of semantics comes the confusion over norms in satire. But satire ranges over the entire field of human activities and relies on standards which may be metaphysical or social or moral.

## THE SATIRIST'S MOTIVATIONS

The satirist is motivated by the aesthetic desire for self-expression far more than by the ethical desire for reform. He is stimulated by the incongruities in society, he is infuriated or amused by them, and he ridicules them. Later, because men are expected to justify their actions, he rationalizes that his purpose was noble and virtuous. It is an understandable rationalization and a pardonable one. But there is not much valuable morality in *Jurgen, Penguin Island, Candide,* or *Brave New World.* Unless one postulates that any attitude toward life is "moral," it is hard to show high ethical purpose in James Cabell's paean to disillusionment, Anatole France's attack on religion, Voltaire's burlesque of [German philosopher] Leibnitz, or Aldous Huxley's *reductio ad absurdum* [disproof of an idea by showing the absurdity of its inevitable conclusion] of scientific planning. It seems likely that the subjects appealed to the authors, as material might strike the fancy of any artist, and that they worked with those subjects to produce art. Having the attitude of satirists, and using the devices most adaptable to satire, they produced the kind of books they did, not to teach a better way of life but primarily to satisfy a creative drive. Satire may be moral, as in [British writer] Samuel Johnson, amoral as in [American critic H.L.] Mencken, or immoral as in [Italian writer] Machiavelli's *Mandragola.*

## UNFAIRNESS OF SATIRE

Satire is unfair. There is no denying this fact, and no need to deny it. The satirist is trying to arouse the attention of men, some of whom are hostile to him and most of whom are completely indifferent. In every society it is the business of established institutions to justify, defend, and glorify the functions of that society. Schools, churches, and governments insist that the society of which they are parts is superior to other societies, that its faults are at worst venial [pardonable], and that its way of life is an excellent one. Popular literature helps to foster the optimistic concept that life is good, cheerful, and rewarding. Some men accept this doctrine. Most men attain, instead, a dull stolidity, a placid acceptance of things as they are, a conviction that reforms or changes are not likely to affect them. Nothing that fails to concern them personally has any perceptible effect on them. They cannot be stirred by imagination or moved by protest, and they make the satirist's task a difficult one.

The satirist, then, has to exaggerate because he is facing formidable opposition: an audience indifferent to expression of unpleasant truths, and a throng of teachers, officials, and writers who insist that these truths do not exist. The modern satirist has to fight the propaganda of television, movies, radio, books, comic strips, newspapers, and popular magazines, all of which, even in democracies, misrepresent reality. *Satire is always unfair.* [Satirists] Byron, Mencken, Rabelais, Juvenal, Pope, Voltaire exaggerate shamelessly. There is no room for fairness in so unequal a struggle as the satirist's against the affectations of orthodoxy. In minimizing goodness, the satirist is no more guilty than the orthodox writers who minimize evil.

The satirist has another good reason for not being fair. To examine carefully the position of one's opponent is to develop a sympathy for him. Since very little in society is all good or all bad, the satirist would find extenuating circumstances in his opponent's situation. To know all is to forgive all. But to be sympathetic is to stop being a satirist. Effective satire cannot be fair and permit [British playwright and novelist] Samuel Beckett to describe life as a progression from "the spermarium to the crematorium."

## SATIRE CANNOT PROVIDE SOLUTIONS

One of the frequent, and absurd, charges made against satire is that it fails to offer satisfactory alternatives for the conditions it criticizes. Why it should be expected to offer these alternatives is difficult to see. On the assumption that only constructive criticism is valuable, no one but a fireman would inform people that a house was burning; no one but a doctor would announce an illness. The mind which sees the faults in society is rarely the kind of mind which visualizes adequate solutions. There is no reason why it should possess two gifts instead of one. It is sufficient to point out faults and let others correct them. A satirist should no more be expected to provide the world with a satisfying way of life than a detective or an exterminator. "My business," said Mencken, "is diagnosis, not therapeutics." He was right. When satirists try to offer alternatives, they usually fail miserably. Both Aldous Huxley and Sinclair Lewis suffer when they imply solutions, the former becoming mystical and the latter banal. The satirist has work to do but planning the ideal society is not part of that work.

## FAMILIAR IDEAS IN NEW FORM

Perhaps the most striking quality of satiric literature is its freshness, its originality of perspective. We are shown old things in a new way. Satire rarely offers original ideas. Instead, it presents the familiar in a new form. Satirists do not offer the world new philosophies. What they do is look at familiar conditions from a perspective which makes these conditions seem foolish, harmful, or affected. Satire jars us out of complacence into a pleasantly shocked realization that many of the values we unquestioningly accept are false. [Miguel de Cervantes'] *Don Quixote* makes chivalry seem absurd; [Aldous Huxley's] *Brave New World* ridicules the pretensions of science; [Swift's] *A Modest Proposal* dramatizes starvation by advocating cannibalism. None of these ideas is original. Chivalry was suspect before Cervantes, humanists objected to the claims of pure science before Aldous Huxley, and Englishmen were aware of famine in Ireland before Swift. It was not the originality of the idea that made these satires popular. It was the manner of expression, the satiric method, which made them interesting and entertaining. Satires are read because they are aesthetically satisfying as works of art, not because they are (as they may be) morally wholesome or ethically instructive. They are stimulating and refreshing because with common-sense briskness they brush away illusions and second-hand opinions. With spontaneous irreverence, satire rearranges perspectives, scrambles familiar objects into incongruous juxtaposition, and speaks in a personal idiom instead of abstract platitude. The vision of life it gives may be unfair but it is fresh and diverting, as when Mencken says,

"Posterity is the penalty of a faulty technique" and [German philosopher Friedrich] Nietzsche mentions "two great European narcotics, alcohol and Christianity."

Satire exists because there is need for it. It has lived because men appreciate a refreshing stimulus, an irreverent reminder that they live in a world of platitudinous thinking, cheap moralizing, and foolish philosophy. Satire serves to prod men into an awareness of truth, though rarely to any action on behalf of truth. Satire tends to remind men that most of what they see, hear, and read in popular media of communication is sanctimonious, sentimental, and only partially true. Life resembles in only a slight degree the popular image of it. Soldiers rarely hold the ideals that movies attribute to them, nor do ordinary men devote their lives to unselfish service of mankind. Intelligent men know these things but tend to forget them when they do not hear them expressed. Satire expresses them in a form pleasant and memorable. "Englishmen," says Shaw, "will never be slaves; they are free to do whatever the government and public opinion allow them to do."

## A Necessary Form of Literature

Satire is not the greatest form of literature but it is a necessary one. It serves a function that the realist and romantic do not fulfill, by dramatizing and exaggerating objectionable qualities in man and society. It does not, and does not try to, give the kind of insight into personality that [novelists] Dostoevsky, Rolland, Tolstoy, and Mann have achieved. A man whose reading was limited to satire would have a perverted vision of life. But so would a man who read only romance or philosophy. It has always been the misfortune of satire to be criticized for failing to do things which it had no intention of doing. No one asks lyric poetry to give a realistic picture of society. No one asks comedy to be introspective. No one requires of the novel that it reform society. Yet all of these demands are made of satire. [American writer] Sinclair Lewis, a satirist who uses exaggeration for comic effects, is criticized for not giving a wholly realistic portrayal of society. Moliére is belittled because his characters do not show the depth and subtlety of William Shakespeare's. Critics repeatedly demand that satire justify its existence by serving a moral purpose. Why should it, any more than any other form of literature? The test for satire is its success within its prescribed sphere. That sphere is criticism of man and society, a criticism made entertaining by humor and moving by irony and invective.

## A PLAYFULLY CRITICAL DISTORTION

Satire is such an amorphous genre that no two scholars define it in the same words. No less an authority than Professor Robert C. Elliott comes to the reluctant conclusion that no satisfactory definition is possible. The best we can do, he suggests, is to look at a number of works traditionally accepted as satires and compare the new work with these examples. If the work we are considering has a reasonable number of resemblances to accepted satires, we are justified in calling it a satiric work. But we should never demand complete conformity to a particular type, and we should accept numerous deviations from familiar practice.

This is a reasonable suggestion. The more one studies satire the more likely he is to permit the widest possible latitude in defining terms. But for purposes of discussing the subject . . . I use this working definition: Satire is a playfully critical distortion of the familiar.

# Swift's World

Philip Pinkus

Jonathan Swift's era was a rapidly changing, tumultuous, war-torn time that produced arguably the finest
satires ever written. Philip Pinkus traces the historical
and philosophical movements during the late seventeenth and eighteenth centuries that led to the creation
of *Gulliver's Travels*. During this era people's conception of the universe and their role in it was changed by
the writings of philosophers such as René Descartes,
Thomas Hobbes and John Locke and by the discoveries
of scientists such as Sir Isaac Newton. The dominant
philosophy of the previous era, Christian humanism,
which centered on living a productive life in order to
remain in God's grace, gave way to a more scientific,
less religious worldview that emphasized humanity's
essential goodness and "man as a creature of society
rather than of God." Philip Pinkus has taught at The
University of British Columbia. He is the author of
*Grub Street Stripped Bare.*

The years from 1660 to 1745, roughly the period of Jonathan
Swift's life, were the heyday of English satire. More satire
and better satire was written then than in any other period
of English literature. It is not easy to explain why this was
so, and many of the reasons are not within the scope of this
introduction. The age did not deserve being satirized more
than any other age, certainly not more than our own world
today. In fact, the age in which Swift lived was probably one
of the most fruitful periods in European history. There are,
however, three main reasons why this was an age of satire.
First, it was a time of radically changing values, when intensely held convictions were in conflict with each other
and a new world order was emerging. Second, a new style of
writing developed that made a most effective satiric instru-
ment. It was the style advocated by the new science which

required a simple, plain, clear, expository vehicle to describe the experiments of the newly-formed Royal Society. As a medium for satire, used in neat, clean strokes, it could cut off a man's head without knocking it from his shoulders—in [English poet John] Dryden's words. When coupled with a forceful imagery, as in Swift's prose, it could hang, draw, and quarter a man, and impale his parts for inspection. In verse, the general medium was the heroic couplet, though Swift's poetry, for the most part, was a bouncing octosyllabic [containing 8 syllables to a line]. The enormous compression of the couplet, its balance and antithesis, gave it, at its best, an exquisitely satiric edge. Third, politicians became aware for the first time that the writer, especially the satirist, could be a powerful weapon against the opposition. Political parties courted him. He acquired new dignity and status and within the close-knit coffee-house society of London where a pamphlet published one day was the talk of the town the next, the satirist's influence was considerable.

## POLITICAL CHANGES IN SWIFT'S AGE

With the Restoration [of King Charles II to the English throne] in 1660 the Civil War did not end, it merely shifted ground. It became a war of pamphlets, and despite the Licensing Act of 1662 the pamphlet war grew to enormous proportions. Every policy had its writer to support it, and every crisis was magnified by the conflict between the rival pamphleteers and newswriters. Since there were many controversies and crises, all concentrated in a relatively small centre of political power, London, the result was a kind of political Bedlam [a famous mental hospital]. First there was the Restoration itself; then the fact that the heir to the throne was Roman Catholic and there was national concern lest the country become Papist, which led to the frenzy of the Popish Plot, the Monmouth Rebellion, the deposition of James II, and the Glorious Revolution of 1688 when William of Orange came to the throne. In the 1680s we have the beginnings of the party system of government with the forming of two opposing political factions, the Whigs and the Tories, each party with its own pamphleteers. A proliferation of Protestant sects confused the scene even further because they were in conflict not only among themselves but with the established Church of England. The sectarians were usually associated with the Whigs and the established church with the Tories, and Whig attempts to remove the civil restrictions of the sectarians brought repeated cries of alarm that the Church was in danger. As for the Roman Catholics, from the time James II was deposed until well on in the eighteenth century they were associated with the Jacobites who wanted to return the Stuarts to the throne and were therefore politically suspect. Throughout this period there were wars: the Thirty Years War (1618–48), the War of Devolution (1667–68), the Dutch War (1672–78), the War of the League of Augsburg (1689–97), the War of the Spanish Succession (1701–13)—almost a century of continual warfare, which spread into the colonial possessions all over the world. The issues of war and peace split the political parties even further. This was the political backdrop against which Swift began writing his satires.

## CHRISTIAN HUMANISM

The frequent political changes of the period were accompanied by a dramatic shift in philosophical and religious attitudes. In the early part of the seventeenth century we may say that, nominally at least, the Christian humanist values of the Renaissance were still the accepted standard. By this standard the activities of daily life were considered not as ends in themselves but as means and judged in moral and ultimately spiritual terms. The purpose of life was to be not merely a good doctor or a lawyer or a skilled craftsman, but a good man and in God's grace. Any endeavour that did not contribute to these ends, any art that did not have an essentially moral and didactic purpose, was fundamentally trivial, if not worse. The ideal was to be a moral, learned, decorous citizen, active in the affairs of one's country, and a good Christian. This was to live the life of reason. For the most part, with some significant qualifications, Swift believed in this ideal to the end of his days.

## "REASON" DEFINED

The word "reason", it will be noticed, does not mean the neat, logical, mathematical "reason" of our own day, or even that of the Age of Reason, as we sometimes call the eighteenth century. It is far more comprehensive than the reason of the Houyhnhnms, in *Gulliver's Travels,* which is a kind of Stoic [indifference to pleasure or pain] common sense. Reason, in this context, is the gift of God to man that enables him to distinguish good from evil and links him to the angelic. The man who conforms to this reason conforms to God. In the largeness of its conception it seemed to suggest the spiritual unity of Renaissance man, a unity that was to be systematically destroyed by an increasing secularism.

## THE PHILOSOPHIES OF DESCARTES AND HOBBES

In 1643 [French philosopher René] Descartes published his *Principles of Philosophy* which denied that matter and spirit were indivisible and conceived of the universe as a mechanical system for which God seemed necessary only as a First Cause. It was a convenient sort of dualism because it provided a logical justification for scholars to study the nature of the physical world without encroaching on religious issues. In 1651 [English philosopher] Thomas Hobbes published the *Leviathan* which asserted that the universe was essentially material, and man himself a creature of appetites, a lump of matter acted upon by the laws of motion. The *Leviathan* was so cogently argued that it could not be ignored. Hobbes became a major force to be reckoned with by every scholar and writer of the period. Much of Swift's [satiric work] *A Tale of a Tub*, especially the Clothes Philosophy of Section II, is an attack on Hobbes's materialism. Then in 1660 the Royal Society was formed. Their method was inductive and experimental. They measured, they dissected; they took a quantitative, mathematical approach to knowledge. But it was the impact of Isaac Newton's discoveries that made ominously clear the implications of their methods. (It should be kept in mind that this analysis is not intended as a comprehensive history of ideas but as a diagram of trends to illustrate an argument.)

## SIR ISAAC NEWTON AND THE END OF IGNORANCE

Newton, by expounding the laws of gravitation, showed how Descartes's machine worked scientifically. The result was that the whole of the physical universe seemed suddenly to open up to man. "God said let Newton be," wrote [English poet] Alexander Pope, "and all was light." There was a tremendous feeling of having triumphed over ages of superstition and ignorance. Though Newton himself was an orthodox Anglican [member of the English church], the implication of his theories was that everything could be penetrated and dissected and understood, given time. There were to be no mysteries, nothing sacred, in the pursuit of scientific investigation.

## JOHN LOCKE'S PHILOSOPHY

Perhaps more than any other single figure, John Locke summed up the outlook of his age and provided the intellectual framework that became the commonplace of the eighteenth century. Like Newton, Locke was a pious man. Yet it was Locke who by emphasizing that reason must be clear and simple and mathematically compelling, and that in this sense Christianity should be a *reasonable* religion, tended to minimize the Christian miracles and the mysteries, even revelation itself. From this point it was only a step to the Deists' [believers in an absentee God] position that revelation was unnecessary and reason alone a sufficient guide in religious matters. Locke's conception of reason led inevitably to the extreme rationalism of [French philosopher Francois] Voltaire which is frequently equated with the Age of Reason—the Age of the Enlightenment.

## A NEW WORLD

With the increasing rationalism and the decline of religious fervour, the orthodox conception of original sin began to lose its hold. In its place a new kind of belief was gaining ground, that man was essentially good, that if left alone he would naturally incline to virtue—virtue being its own reward and not requiring the Christian system of rewards and punishments to be made desirable. By emphasizing man's essential goodness there was less need for divine grace. Man had his own intrinsic worth as a creature of society rather than of God. This is the basis of the literary movement known as sentimentalism. We are on our way to the democratic assertion of the rights of man and the French Revolution.

From all these factors it is evident that a new world was evolving, a world of empirical [based on observation or experiment] values, whose conception of reality was not the supernatural but the secular, physical world that can be seen and touched, the external, quantitative, mathematical world that we live in today. In this period, the intellectual conception of the world as we know it was formed.

Swift spent most of his life fighting the inevitable trend of history, pointing his satire at the secular, mechanical tendencies of the new order. He felt more and more, as he grew older, that the spiritual light of the world was going out. This helps to explain the difference in intensity between the exuberance of *A Tale of a Tub* (1704) and the exasperation of *Gulliver's Travels* (1726); the increasingly pessimistic utterances of his last years; and the legend of the gloomy Dean, the dark, forbidding figure of St. Patrick's Cathedral, Dublin, which grew around him even in his lifetime.

# The Enthusiastic Reception of *Gulliver's Travels*

A.L. Rowse

In his biography, *Jonathan Swift*, A.L. Rowse recounts how Swift first conceived of writing *Gulliver's Travels*. While the book is often thought of as a children's story, it is, ironically, a savage indictment of human society, which Swift wrote more to "vex" than to entertain his readers. Swift detested humanity en masse; individuals he could care for, but society filled him with contempt. *Gulliver's Travels* is built upon this misanthropic worldview. The publication of the book caused something of a sensation in England. Swift deliberately published it anonymously, which led to the impression among some that Gulliver was a real man. Rowse quotes liberally from a letter by Swift's friend, Dr. John Arbuthnot, to suggest the widespread delight with which most readers first read *Gulliver's Travels*. A.L. Rowse, who died in 1997, taught at Oxford University in England and was a senior fellow at the Huntington Library in California. He was the author of over ninety books, including several on Jonathan Swift.

Where *A Tale of a Tub* is an English classic, *Gulliver's Travels* is a world classic. It has been read all over the world for its story and its fantasy, particularly the first two books, dealing with Lilliput, where everything is on a minute scale so that Gulliver appears as a giant, and Brobdingnag, where the inhabitants are on the scale of giants and he is a mere manikin. The extraordinary controlled imagination that could carry through two such projects—one seeing everything through a microscopic lens, the other through an enormous magnifying glass—has never ceased to appeal. People think of them as children's stories, and they have

Excerpted from *Jonathan Swift* by A.L. Rowse (New York: Scribner's). Copyright © 1975 by A.L. Rowse. Reprinted with the permission of Curtis Brown Ltd.

been reproduced scores of times as such. Even Part IV, the kingdom where horses rule, has not been without its popular appeal, suitably edited and censored, for the horse is a noble animal and everybody likes horses. Part III, the voyage to Laputa with the flying island attached, has always been the least popular and is of a more specialized interest; for myself, I find it the funniest, it makes me laugh more than the other books.

The fate and fortune of this masterpiece is not the least of the ironies in the life of this strange man. For what is read as a children's story is the most savage satire written upon human society and upon man himself; and Swift wrote it less to give pleasure than, as he said, to vex mankind. . . .

## THE GENESIS OF *GULLIVER'S TRAVELS*

The idea of the book went back to the Scriblerus Club, of which Swift was the leading spirit, which was formed in that last winter in London, 1713–14. [Swift's friend John] Arbuthnot, Alexander Pope, John Gay and Thomas Parnell were the other members. They were to write the memoirs of their joint creation, [the fictional writer] Martin Scriblerus. The project did not get very far. Arbuthnot reported to Swift, in his withdrawal to Letcombe [in the English countryside], 'to talk of Martin in any hands but yours is a folly. You every day give better hints than all of us together could do in a twelvemonth. Pope, who first thought of the hint, has no genius at all to it in my mind. Gay is too young; Parnell has some ideas of it, but is idle.' Arbuthnot was to write up the medicine, Swift a voyage and 'the projects of Laputa'—'all that relates to the sciences must be from you.'

## WILLIAM DAMPIER'S TRAVELS

The idea germinated in Swift's mind. Voyages made popular reading throughout the reign of Queen Anne, the most remarkable being those of William Dampier, a West Countryman who had an astonishing career in all the oceans as seaman, buccaneer, pirate and excellent hydrographer. Anyone who has read his *Voyages*—two of them dedicated to members of the Whig Junto [English political party], one of them Swift's disappointing patron, [Lord] Halifax, the other, Orford [*sic:* the Earl of Oxford, Sir Robert Harley]—will recognize the use Swift made of them. The style Swift adhered to was Dampier's plain, factual, nautical reporting; at one point

## An Animal Capable of Reason

*In a famous letter to his friend, the poet Alexander Pope, Swift redefines man as an animal capable of reason, and not a reasoning animal.*

Sep. 29, 1725

I have employd my time (besides ditching) in finishing correcting, amending, and Transcribing my Travells, in four parts Compleat newly Augmented, and intended for the press when the world shall deserve them, or rather when a Printer shall be found brave enough to venture his Eares, . . . the chief end I propose to my self in all my labors is to vex the world rather then divert it, and if I could compass that designe without hurting my own person or Fortune I would be the most Indefatigable writer you have ever seen without reading. . . .

I have ever hated all Nations professions and Communityes and all my love is towards individualls for instance I hate the tribe of Lawyers, but I love Councellor such a one, Judge such a one for so with Physicians (I will not Speak of my own Trade) Soldiers, English, Scotch, French; and the rest but principally I hate and detest that animal called man, although I hartily love John, Peter, Thomas and so forth. this is the system upon which I have governed my self many years (but do not tell) and so I shall go on till I have done with them I have got Materials Towards a Treatis proving the falsity of that Definition *animal rationale* [rational animal]; and to show it should be only *rationis capax* [capable of reason]. Upon this great foundation of Misanthropy (though not Timons manner) The whole building of my Travells is erected: And I never will have peace of mind till all honest men are of my Opinion: by Consequence you are to embrace it immediatly and procure that all who deserve my Esteem may do so too. The matter is so clear that it will admit little dispute. nay I will hold a hundred pounds that you and I agree in the Point.

Jonathan Swift, *The Correspondence of Jonathan Swift*, Vol. III. Oxford: Clarendon, 1963, pp. 102–04.

there is a full-page parody of his hydrographical detail. The maps that accompanied *Gulliver's Travels* are designed to give verisimilitude.

Dampier's voyage to the East Indies and the north coast of Australia took place in 1699; Lilliput and Blefuscu are charted way off in the Indian Ocean from Sumatra and Van Diemen's Land (Tasmania), as discovered in 1699. Dampier was in the Pacific in 1703; Brobdingnag is described as 'dis-

covered A.D. 1703', it is attached to North America, where
Alaska is, beyond the fabled Straits of Anian, north of California, which is given Sir Francis Drake's name, New Albion.
Laputa, Balnibarbi and Lugnagg, lie in the Pacific off Japan,
'discovered 1701'. 'Houyhnhnm Land' was 'discovered A.D.
1711'—this was the year in which Dampier returned from
his voyage round the world, having rescued [marooned Scot-
tish sailor Alexander] Selkirk from his solitary confinement
on Juan Fernandez. This was the inspiration of Defoe's
*Robinson Crusoe,* published in 1719, which had such success
that further installments were demanded.

## Swift Commences *Gulliver's Travels*

Swift was not long in following suit. During the years 1722–4
he was comparatively free of his old complaint in his head,
giddiness and deafness. [Swift's friend Charles] Ford was his
confidant in regard to writing and publishing *Gulliver;*
Swift's first reference to it is in April 1721, 'I am now writing
a history of my Travels, which will be a large volume, and
gives account of countries hitherto unknown; but they go on
slowly for want of health and humour.' With the recovery of
his health the pace picked up; the first two books were written in 1721–2; then the fourth book in 1723. Ford must have
told [English statesman and friend, Henry] Bolingbroke,
'else how should he know anything of Stella or of Horses. I
would have him and you know that I hate Yahoos of both
sexes, and that Stella [Swift's love interest] and Madame de
Villette [Bolingbroke's mistress and subsequent wife] are
only tolerable at best for want of Houhyhnhnms.' This was
in January 1724: "I have left the Country of Horses and am
in the Flying Island [this was the original order in which
Swift wrote these sections], where I shall not stay long, and
my two last journeys will be soon over.'

In August 1725, he writes from Quilca [a country house],
'I have finished my Travels and I am now transcribing them.
They are admirable things, and will wonderfully mend the
world.' He was staying there in [English writer Richard]
Sheridan's parsonage with the ladies, 'reading books twice
over for want of fresh ones, and fairly correcting and transcribing my Travels for the public.' It would seem that he
was reading [Cervantes' novel] *Don Quixote*; while next
month he is advising the too confiding Sheridan, 'expect no
more from man than such an animal is capable of, and you

will every day find my description of Yahoos more resembling.'

## SWIFT'S PRINCIPLES OF MISANTHROPY

To Pope he imparted the principles of his misanthropy, the foundation upon which 'the whole building is erected . . . I have ever hated all nations, professions, and communities, and all my love is towards individuals. For instance, I hate the tribe of lawyers, but I love Councillor Such-a-one, and Judge Such-a-one. So with physicians—I will not speak of my own trade—soldiers, English, Scotch, French, and the rest. But principally I hate and detest the animal called man, although I heartily love John, Peter, Thomas and so forth.'

In short, the Dean was not a Christian but—like that other Anglo-Irishman of genius, Lawrence of Arabia—a Manichee [a believer in Manicheanism, a philosophy that divides the world into good and evil].

In other words, what he detested was Mass-Man—and he had this on his side, that human beings are always to be seen at their most idiotic in their mass-behaviour, as members of the herd, whether nations or churches, political parties, trade unions or, for that matter, universities, even when the individual in himself may be reasonable enough, at times. What Swift detested was the nonsensical belief that men as a whole were rational—their behaviour showed that this was not true. At the utmost, they were capable of reason; then why don't they act on it more? That is the question.

It is really a very complex question, more complex than Swift, who had settled for a rather simple rationalism, perhaps realized—it was another Anglo-Irishman, Edmund Burke, who realized more fully the subtlety of it. Anyhow, the evidences of men's refusal to use what reason they have got were all round him, especially in Ireland, and Swift was right to highlight the evidences of their idiocy. He was a moralist and preacher: he was right to bring home to them again and again the consequences of their folly—how otherwise can, or will, the fools learn? Some of them can learn something some of the time; very well, they should be made to, and if they refuse, they should be lashed for it—it is probable that they understand that better. 'When you think of the world give it one lash the more at my request. The chief end I propose in all my labours is to vex the world rather than divert it.'. . .

Swift may be said to have loved virtue, and recognized it in a man when he saw it. 'Oh! if the world had but a dozen Arbuthnots in it, I would burn my Travels.' As it was, by September 1725 they were ready for the press, 'when the world shall deserve them, or rather when a printer shall be found brave enough to venture his ears.' That in itself should show that the political and social implications of the book were what Swift thought most important about it. 'Drown the world! I am not content with despising it, but I would anger it, if I could with safety. I wish there were an hospital built for its despisers, where one might act with safety, and it need not be a large building, only I would have it well endowed.' He was in time to endow such a building with his life's savings—it would be a lunatic asylum. . . .

## PUBLICATION

Nothing remained now but the publication of *Gulliver's Travels,* upon which Swift embarked with more than the usual amount of mystification. He was genuinely apprehensive that ministers would take offence at the political satire and personal references—what he later described as 'the sting' of the book. And indeed the printer took the liberty, in these circumstances, of toning it down, and even inserting mollifying passages—about which Swift complained bitterly later. Though his habit was not to receive money for his writings, he stipulated for the considerable sum of £200 for this, his masterpiece.

Having set the printing of the book in motion, through intermediaries and via the pseudonym of 'Richard Sympson', he departed for Ireland in August, . . .

## RECEPTION

Soon the news came over the water of the tremendous hit the book made—as [English writer] Dr [Samuel] Johnson said, 'a production so new and so strange filled the reader with a mingled emotion of merriment and amazement. Criticism was, for a while, lost in wonder.' For a time the mystification as to its authorship added to the *réclame* [advertisement]; Swift himself kept up the farce of not recognizing it, and only a few people at first were in the know. His friends reported how people were taking it. When Arbuthnot went to see the Princess [of Wales, Caroline] 'she was reading *Gulliver* and was just come to the passage of the hobbling

Prince, which she laughed at.' There was no difficulty in recognizing the bearing of that passage. The acrimonious party dispute in Lilliput was between High-Heels and Low-Heels, i.e. High Church v. Low Church. . . .

. . . The joke about heels was carried on in the Princess's circle, as we observe from Swift's correspondence.

Arbuthnot goes on, '*Gulliver* is in everybody's hands. Lord Scarborough fell in company with a master of a ship, who told him that he was very well acquainted with Gulliver, but that he lived in Wapping and not in Rotherhithe. I lent the book to an old gentleman, who went immediately to his map to search for Lilliput.' An Irish bishop was much wiser: he said that the book was full of improbable lies, and 'for his part, he hardly believed a word of it'.

The reaction of the old Duchess of Marlborough was much to her credit, after all that Swift had written against the Duke. 'She says she can dream of nothing else since she read it. She declares that she has now found out that her whole life has been lost in caressing the worst part of mankind, and treating the best as her foes. If she knew Gulliver, though he had been the worst enemy she ever had, she would give up her present acquaintance for his friendship.' It must not be supposed that the old Duchess had any more justice of mind than Swift had, even less; her enthusiasm was partly due to the fact that she too had moved over to the opposition against her former *protégé*, [British Prime Minister Sir Robert] Walpole. We see how personal spite enters into people's judgments, even remarkable people, who should know better.

Some of the party politicians felt themselves touched, even among Swift's friends. Lord Harcourt thought 'in some places the matter too far carried'—but he was a stuffed shirt. Lord Bolingbroke 'is the person who least approves it, blaming it as a design of evil consequence to depreciate human nature; at which it cannot be wondered that he takes most offence, being himself the most accomplished of his species.' This was good-humoured irony; but, in fact, the political gambler, who had gambled away the whole future of his party at the end of Queen Anne's reign [1702–1714], was now engaged in making for himself a second career as a benevolent philosopher, and could not accept Swift's view of human nature. . . .

The generality of people were delighted, since they had

not the sense to know what the motive was. Pope and Gay reported that the book 'has been the conversation of the whole town' ever since its publication. 'The whole impression [printing] sold in a week, and nothing is more diverting than to hear the different opinions people give of it, though all agree in liking it extremely. It is generally said that you are the author; but I am told the bookseller declares he knows not from what hand it came. From the highest to the lowest it is universally read, from the cabinet-council to the nursery.'

Like all universal books, it has always retained that width of appeal. Arbuthnot, judicious as ever, summed it up: '*Gulliver's Travels*, I believe, will have as great a run as John Bunyan [author of *A Pilgrim's Progress,* the most popular book of its time].'

# Gulliver's Travels and Robinson Crusoe

Nigel Dennis

No book had a more profound effect on *Gulliver's Travels* than Daniel Defoe's famous tale of a shipwrecked businessman, *Robinson Crusoe*. Though it might be too strong to describe Swift's book as a deliberate answer to Defoe, the two works stand in almost complete opposition to each other. Crusoe's ability to survive on a deserted island celebrates the triumph of human ingenuity, while Swift roasts humanity with his savagely satiric pen. These conflicting beliefs are clearly suggested in each book's ending. Crusoe returns triumphantly to find "that the world is good," whereas Gulliver comes back to a world that he believes is populated by "stinking Yahoos." Nigel Dennis's books include *Jonathan Swift: A Short Character, Exotics: Poems of the Mediterranean and Middle East* and *An Essay on Malta.*

A great deal has been written about . . . [*Gulliver's Travels*] originating in the ideas and table-talk of Swift and his London friends, but without questioning the correctness of this ascription, must we not also allow *Robinson Crusoe*, which appeared in 1719, some of the honour of having set it going? We cannot do so with any firmness, unfortunately, but we can certainly use the one book as a point of departure for the other; for the two, seen side by side, form a wonderful pair, representing two sorts of writing, two entirely disparate views of fiction and two superbly opposed authors. To describe *Gulliver's Travels* as Swift's deliberate retort to *Robinson Crusoe* would be unwarranted, but if we amuse ourselves by considering it as such, the result is as informative as it is entertaining. Moreover, we never see Swift more clearly than in relation to Defoe: each demands the presence of the other, in the sense that each side demands the presence of the other if we are to understand a battle, a Parliamentary conflict, a divided nation.

## SWIFT AND DEFOE AS OPPOSITES

Defoe embodies everything that Swift hates: he is the other half of England that Swift struggled all his life to suppress or ignore and by which he was defeated and driven into isolation. Defoe, with his brickworks and bankruptcies, is the rising small business man whom Swift saw very correctly as the man who would unseat his timocracy [a state governed on principles of honor and military glory] of landed gentlemen and substitute an economy of stocks and shares for one of estate and title. He is the Roundhead Dissenter [Puritan faction during English Civil War] to whom the Whigs run as an ally in their fight with the Tories of the Established Church—and, by turning to him, change what was formerly a private quarrel between Anglican landlords into a lasting division between regicide [king killing] Puritan merchants and honourable county squires. Swift is the gentleman-author whose chosen home is society and the dignified sphere of the well-educated and well-born; Defoe is the born gander of Grub Street [world of literary hacks], the father of all that is noisiest and freest in modern journalism. Defoe is liberty in the form in which Swift detested it most: he is the rogue whom Swift loved best to "swinge", and his life is a constant, rapscallionly muddle, bursting with excitements and devoid of all dignity. Where Swift goes in danger of the Tower [of London; dissident prison], Defoe's natural punishment is the pillory: the higher place is reserved for the treasonable gentleman, the lower for the provocative hack. The two men have only three things in common: the first is that they both took service under Harley [British politician], Swift as unpaid propagandist and Defoe as paid informer; the second is that they were both passionately in favour of the educating of women; and the third is that both were capable of satire. We expect satire from a Tory like Swift, but we are surprised and interested to find it in an enthusiastic Whig. Yet Defoe's *The Shortest Way with the Dissenters,* the satirical essay for which he was put in the pillory, anticipates exactly in tone and tendency Swift's *Modest Proposal* for dealing with surplus Irishmen: the only real difference between the two essays is that Defoe's makes its plea for the mutilating of Dissenters in rather a blunt way, whereas Swift's plea for eating babies [in "A Modest Proposal"] is made with the refinement and gentility that we expect from a clergyman of the better class.

Of the two Defoe is by far the more sympathetic and agreeable man and fits most happily today into the excessively unaustere society that composes our democracy. He is the beginning of the social struggle of which we are the end, and he presses forward into modern times proportionately as Swift fights backwards into the time behind him. When we hold each man's masterpiece in our hands we hold the halves of one apple—the apple of discord that, in its wholeness, represents the England of the early eighteenth century.

### *ROBINSON CRUSOE*

Robinson Crusoe has been called aptly "the primary textbook of capitalism"—and who can resist the amusement of reading it as such? What author ever built such a warehouse or drew up a more satisfying inventory? Every page is a merchant's catalogue of hardware, woollens, leather goods and crockery, and from the fields outside the warehouse come the baaing of the good tradesman's flocks and the ripple of the breeze through his stalks of corn. All these goods, together with a snug house fenced and barricaded interminably against burglars, are available to the forceful capitalist, who, by diligent sowing of a little seed, builds his frugal investments into interest-bearing property. And how excitedly we labour with Crusoe, first for mere self-survival, later for a higher rate of interest and greater abundance of possessions! How we share his horrified terror when that most magical of all moments in fiction, the footprint in the sand, tells us brutally that some barbarous intruder threatens not only life but property! And how thankful we are to know that our heroic investor does not stand alone—that his marvels of free enterprise are noted and sanctioned by God Himself! For, certainly, there never was a book in which God's hand was busier—helping in the factory, making sound economical suggestions, keeping an eye on things generally and asking nothing in return but prayers—heart-felt prayers, of course; but who would *not* pray heartily to such a generous Father? No Puritan but [English writer John] Bunyan ever wrote a happier book; no merchant ever looked upon his gains and declared with greater self-satisfaction that the earth was the Lord's and the glory thereof.

## CONTRASTING *ROBINSON CRUSOE* AND *GULLIVER'S TRAVELS*

At the time *Robinson Crusoe* appeared Swift was reading all the travel books he could find: they were all trash but a perfect antidote to the spleen [ill temper], he assured [his friend] Miss Vanhomrigh. Merely to imagine him reading *Robinson Crusoe* is enough to make one laugh, for it is pleasing to picture his contemptuous response to Defoe's unceasing power to declare, in all imaginable matters, his faith in all that Swift despised. Each author, to begin with, sets out upon his "Travels" with the intention of discovering only that which he already knows and erecting in a strange land that which he knows to have been built at home. Defoe turns a primitive island into a commercial enterprise: the only enemy to this sort of civilization is the naked savage—the terrifying cannibal whose primitive appetites threaten disaster to the God-fearing businessman. But Swift's islands are never menaced by barbarism: on the contrary, the only atrocities he finds are those of civilized, cultured persons who have degenerated grossly from the happier, natural state of man and have espoused reason only in order that "the corruption of that faculty might be worse than brutality itself". Where Defoe looks with horror at the naked footprint, Swift looks with equal horror at the imprint of the court-shoe, and Gulliver, even after being wounded by savages, would still prefer "to trust myself among those barbarians, than live with European Yahoos". The Dissenting merchant and reformer never doubts that trade and colonization confer civilized benefits upon savage people: it is the Tory churchman who argues, with the modern radical, that colonists are no better than an "execrable crew of butchers" enjoying "a free license . . . to all acts of inhumanity and lust".

Man himself, as he walks the world, drives the two authors to opposite poles. Defoe will have no truck with the naked body; his excitements come from the fabricating of its garments out of the available raw materials and from its foodstuffs and implements. But the High Church Dean [Swift] despises "the subject of . . . diet, wherewith other travellers fill their books", and where Defoe asks that we admire the fur hat and skin-breeches Swift keeps pulling off these contemptible disguises and pressing our eyes and noses to the hairy warts and stenches of the flesh below. The Puritan is far too respectable even to mention the functions of the body, but the

Dean's book abounds in hogsheads of urine and the voiding of excrement. This is why *Robinson Crusoe* is an essentially materialistic book and yet a wholly unphysical one, whereas *Gulliver's Travels* is only occasionally materialistic and always passionately physical.

The numerous other "opposites" in the two books are all very engaging and highly characteristic of their respective authors. Crusoe is a simple man of Defoe's own class; Gulliver, like Sir William Temple [Swift's mentor], is a graduate of Emmanuel College, Cambridge. Unlike Defoe's God, the Dean's is much too detached and Olympian to be involved in Gulliver's absurd affairs—and Gulliver himself is much too much an average gentleman to waste a moment in prayer. The Dissenter [Defoe], once he has built himself a small realm abroad, delights in allowing "liberty of conscience throughout my dominions"; the Dean [Swift], however, does not lose the opportunity of requiring the monarch of Brobdignag to assert that "a man may be allowed to keep poisons in his closet, but not to vend them about for cordials".

But the most entertaining contrast between the books, from a literary point of view, is in each author's declared intention. *Robinson Crusoe* is the work of a journalist; it is essentially what we would call a "documentary", or a blunt unpolished recital of the plain facts—yet it is of this documentary that Defoe says: "My story is a whole collection of wonders". *Gulliver's Travels*, on the other hand, *is* a whole collection of wonders—as much an imaginary creation as *Crusoe* is not and, for the most part, most admirably "turned"and polished. Yet Swift declares of it: "I could perhaps, like others, have astonished thee with strange, improbable tales; but I rather chose to relate plain matter of fact, in the simplest manner and style. . . ." Thus does each author indulge the perfectly excusable pretence that suits his book, the journalist seeking to elevate his facts into fancy, the wit to resolve pure fantasy into facts.

*Robinson Crusoe*, one may say, never gets off the ground at all: it is rarely touched by the imagination and asks nothing of the intellect. But *Gulliver's Travels* is a work of pure intellect, an act of unceasing invention. Defoe, patiently assembling material facts, needs forty pages of preliminaries to wreck his hero on a desert island; Swift, anxious to leave the factual world behind, carries Gulliver to Lilliput in little more than a page. Defoe, having retailed one fact, merely goes on to retail the next fact; but the chief purpose served by a fact in Swift is to be a spring-board into fantasy. And nothing about *Gulliver's Travels* is more interesting than to study the way in which this fantasy is anchored—to see why, even at its most fantastic moments, it does not lose its ties with the earth. To see how Swift does this, is to see what satire must always do if its angry fantasies are to be brought safely home.

## THE HUMAN BODY IN *GULLIVER'S TRAVELS*

[The French Emperor] Napoleon, discussing at St. Helena [the island that was Napoleon's last home] the innovations of the French Revolution, declared himself entirely in favour of the change made by the revolutionary intellectuals to the Metric System of weights and measures. But he pointed out that the mathematicians who arranged this change made a typical academic mistake: by throwing away the old *terms*, they turned weights and measures into inhuman abstractions. The man who works with a terminology of *hands, feet* and *ells* in effect bases all his calculations on the parts of his body: even when he speaks in terms of *poles* and *chains*, he is still speaking of what he regards as extensions of his own arms. But once he must calculate in *ares* and *metres*, he must lose his

### FANTASTIC VOYAGES BEFORE *GULLIVER'S TRAVELS*

Gulliver's Travels *falls within the genre of the imaginary voyage. Numerous European writers had written exotic fictional travel tales before Swift.*

Although there are a number of English candidates as models for Swift's mixture of dystopia and utopia in the fantastic lands visited by Gulliver, from Sir Thomas More's *Utopia* (1516) and Bishop Joseph Hall's *Discovery of a New World* (1609) to Henry Neville's *Isle of Pines* (1668) and *Robinson Crusoe* (1719), and although it is possible to go back to classical sources such as Lucian, (flourished second century A.D.) and his *True Story*, a satire on lying tales of adventure, the imaginary voyage was predominantly a form developed by the French. Rabelais's *Gargantua and Pantagruel* concludes with a voyage to strange lands on an impossible quest, and in his mid-seventeenth-century voyages to the sun and moon Cyrano de Bergerac (1619–55) set up the pattern of journeying to worlds where merely being a human being was evidence enough for the inhabitants of those regions to put a voyager on trial for cruelty and viciousness. De Bergerac's tendency toward deism is carried forward in two other imaginary sense of physical conjunction with the world, and the loss of this sensuous tie, Napoleon believed, was precisely the sort of loss that always should be avoided in the modernising of ancient systems.

In this spasm of light from a dying star we see clearly one of the great strengths of *Gulliver's Travels*—the anchoring of the high-flying mind to the physical body. This is not the book of an abstract "projector" calculating in a world apart; it is a book in which man *is* the measure of all things. We find this first, of course, in the simple matter of relative sizes in Lilliput and Brobdignag, but it is the actual estimating of these proportions—the terms in which they are assessed—that is so unabstract and gives the book its fleshy solidity. Like Defoe, Swift will often tell us how small or large a thing was by giving its linear measurement; but, unlike Defoe, he prefers to lay a human limb alongside it, to make his comparison, and to press our eyes, noses and ears into the service of his imaginings. In the huge magnifications of Brobdignag, the purring of a cat is not described in mere adjectival sonorities; instead, it is "like that of a dozen stockingweavers at work". A gigantic infant's cry is "a squall that you might have heard from Lon-

voyages that were translated into English and widely read: Gabriel de Foigny's (c. 1650–92) travels to the land of the winged hermaphrodites, and Denis Vairasse's (*fl.* 1665–81) discovery of a wise and deistical race known as the Severambes. Foigny's work was translated in 1693 and Vairasses's, though first translated in 1675–79, was popular enough to receive a second translation in the eighteenth century (1716). Both of these works preserved a sense of realism at the start in imitation of the many accounts of genuine voyages to newly-discovered lands that seemed only slightly less amazing than these deliberate fantasies. The Accounts of William Dampier (1652–1715) begun in 1697 but not finished until 1709 and of Woodes Rogers (?–1732) published in 1712 were read with delight by a large audience. Rogers's account of the rescue of Alexander Selkirk, who had been living in isolation on the island of Juan Fernandez, attracted the attention of Sir Richard Steele and, even more significantly, Daniel Defoe, who was to use a number of details from Selkirk's experiences for *Robinson Crusoe*.

Maximillian E. Novak, *Eighteenth-Century English Literature*. New York: Schocken, 1983, pp. 86–7.

don Bridge to Chelsea"; and twenty wasps, "as large as partridges", sweep in at the window "humming louder than the drone of as many bagpipes". The Brobdignagian queen can "craunch the wing of a lark, bones and all, between her teeth, although it were nine times as large as that of a full-grown turkey", and her table knives are "twice as long as a scythe". Each fly is of the greatness of "a Dunstable lark" and, as it walks, demonstrates its essential monstrousness to the eye of the tiny observer by leaving behind it a loathsome trail of excrement, spawn and "viscous matter". One paring from the Queen's thumbnail serves for the back of a horn comb, bladed with "stumps of the King's beard"; the corn on the toe of a royal maid-of-honour is of "about the bigness of a Kentish pippin"; sliced from its owner and carried home to England, it can be "hollowed into a cup, and set in silver". Waves of overpowering stench and scent are emitted by the naked bodies of those royal maids, and each charming mole that spots the skin stands "broad as a trencher, and hairs hanging from it thicker than packthreads". The thump on the scaffold floor of a murderer's decapitated head is such as to shake the ground for "at least half an English mile", while—most astonishing simile of all—the "veins and arteries [of the trunk] spouted up such a prodigious quantity of blood, and so high in the air, that the great *jet d'eau* at Versailles was not equal for the time it lasted". Reversed in their proportions to fit the world of Lilliput, the similes are more charming than gross, but they always retain their intense, familiar quality—tiny men ploughing through Gulliver's snuff-box "up to the mid-leg in a sort of dust" and sneezing dreadfully as they go; examining letters and diaries in which every character is "almost half as large as the palm of our hands"; discovering a pocket-watch, "which the emperor was very curious to see, and commanded two of his tallest yeoman of the guards to bear it on a pole upon their shoulders, as draymen in England do a barrel of ale". "I have been much pleased", says Gulliver, "with a cook pulling a lark, which was not so large as a common fly; and a young girl threading an invisible needle with invisible silk".

## SWIFT USES THE NICEST AND NASTIEST IMAGERY

This intense proximity, this use of commonplaces to ground the imagination, has a curious effect. It is not noticed by the reader when he finds it pleasing: he merely smiles at the image without inquiring into the techniques that have made him smile. But when the simile is gross—when excrement and hairy moles replace invisible needles and snuff—he not only sees the technique but begins to wonder what sort of man the author was. Yet it should be plain that the same method is being used throughout and that there is a grand unity of treatment that covers in one way the nicest and nastiest things. For every grossness in Swift there is a corresponding delicacy—a point nicely made by [English poet Alexander] Pope in his well-known lines on Swift. But whichever course, fine or gross, he chooses to take, an intensely personal intimacy lies at the core of it. The grand flights of his imagination are made plausible only by the point from which they take their departure, and this point is always the living human being and his familiar belongings, sensations and habits. Nor is there any limit to the use of this admirable art; it can be applied not only to the coarsest and most delicate things but also to the occasions when genius displays itself by listing details in the simplest way and then turning them, without the least change of expression, to irresistibly human account:

> ". . . Their manner of writing is very peculiar, being neither from the left to the right, like the Europeans; nor from the right to the left, like the Arabians; nor from up to down, like the Chinese; but aslant, from one corner of the paper to the other, like ladies in England."

The life we share with Robinson Crusoe has no place for such extraordinary felicities. It is, in the friendliest sense of the words, merely a life of gain, technical security, adventure and everyday ingenuity; it provides neither insight into human behaviour nor interest in human thought. *Gulliver's Travels* begins where *Robinson Crusoe* ends; it enquires and reflects where the other rests content to act and possess. We see Crusoe naked only when he is afraid, but we see Gulliver in all his human weaknesses—in his fear, his vanity, his pride, his shame, his shivering little skin. Neither Gulliver nor Crusoe is of much interest as a principal character, but each is uninteresting for a different reason—Crusoe because his material possessions loom larger than he does, Gulliver because his story would have no solid centre if he himself were made as dramatically extraordinary as the situations and persons he meets: in this respect we may compare him to the plain Martin in [Swift's] *A Tale of a Tub*. We ask that Gulliver be a bigger man only for one reason—we cannot forgive him for surrendering to the Houyhnhnms and recognising in himself and us the beastly image of a Yahoo. And we do not forgive him for this because we shall never forgive Swift for it.

## CONCLUSIONS OF THE TWO WORKS

A good way to examine this matter is to compare good-humouredly the conclusions of *Robinson Crusoe* and *Gulliver's Travels*. In both books, the hero is carried safe back to Europe by a kindly ship's captain, a Portuguese in Gulliver's case, an Englishman in Crusoe's. We know the revulsion that the return to the world excites in Gulliver—how he shrinks from the touch of his own wife and children, how repugnant he finds the stench and character of the Yahoo. But we should remember, too, how different the world seems to Defoe's returning castaway. Crusoe finds that the world is good—indeed, that it is overflowing with probity and justice. The twenty-eight years of his absence have been devoted by his honest partners to the preservation and increase of his investments, and the totting up of the grand total, with the occasional pause for an *Ave Maria* [Hail Mary], forms a most suitable conclusion to this best of mercantile books. Twelve hundred chests of sugar, 800 rolls of tobacco, thousands of golden Portuguese moidores [gold coins], large Brazilian plantations worked assiduously by black slaves: it all amounts to "above £5,000 sterling" and a South American estate of "above £1,000 a year". And when we hear the chink of those moidores, do we not exclaim with Crusoe: "It is impossible to express the flutterings of my very heart when I looked over these letters and especially when I found all my wealth about me"? Do we not agree most heartily with him that "the latter end of Job was better than the beginning"? And are we at all surprised to find Job in that *galère?*

This is the happy end we all want—honest men, a banker-God, and accumulated interest. Defoe never denied it even to the worst of us: once Moll Flanders [character in a Defoe work of the same name] stopped being a whore and a thief and invested in probity and God, her income rose in due proportion with her piety, cementing the delights of capital to the forgiveness of sins. And because we feel that things *should* turn out like this in a novel—that money is what Job is being so patient about; that money is what Swift loses when [his friend] Miss Vanhomrigh dies—we are profoundly offended when Gulliver shrinks from touching us, and his author, peeling us down to mere skin and claws, wipes us from his sight as stinking Yahoos. His terrible insult has survived two centuries unimpaired: it hurts us today even more than it hurt its first readers. Many, indeed, protest that no author who really believed in God could find it in his heart to condemn us so unkindly; others, more expert in the study of Swift, have turned the insult by tracing it to a psychological deformation in the author. All of which has one very amusing result—that we regard *Robinson Crusoe*, which is a documentary, as an acceptable piece of fiction, but dismiss *Gulliver's Travels*, which is a pure fiction, as a libellous piece of documentary. Yet this absurd conclusion suits both authors admirably, for Defoe, as has been noted, pretended to be a teller of wonders, while Swift pretended to be a reporter of facts. The journalist set out to please his public; the Dean intended to roast it. Both authors succeeded admirably in their intentions, and both are read still in the spirit in which they wrote. Both would be overjoyed to know it.

# Swift's Satire of English Politics

Matthew Hodgart

While several of Jonathan Swift's earlier works changed English politics and practices, *Gulliver's Travels* is notable for its lack of any practical influence. Yet, *Gulliver's Travels* survives as a book with wide and universal satiric significance, very much as Swift intended it. Nevertheless, Swift's satire of contemporary English politics is found almost everywhere in the travels. In this excerpt from *Satire*, Matthew Hodgart identifies the specific political targets Swift had in mind in each of the four parts of *Gulliver's Travels*. Matthew Hodgart has taught at Cambridge College in England. He has written several books on Irish novelist James Joyce, and one imaginative work entitled *A new voyage to the country of the Houyhnhnms: being the fifth part of the travels into several remote parts of the world by Lemuel Gulliver, first a surgeon and then a captain of several ships, wherein the author returns and finds a new state of liberal horses and revolting Yahoos, from an unpublished manuscript.*

Swift had been highly successful as a propagandist in his *Conduct of the Allies*, which more by persuasive argument than by satire had helped to win over the [lower house of English Parliament] House of Commons to accepting the [English Conservative Party] Tory Peace of Utrecht in 1713; and again in his *Drapier's Letters*, in which he took up the cause of the Irish. Single-handed he defeated the English government over a matter of currency reform, and became a hero of the dissident Dubliners: this was a reversion to the cruder methods of [the period after 1660] Restoration satire, including the satirical ballad, and worked very well in a revolutionary situation. But his masterpiece, *Gulliver's Travels*, had no perceptible influence on the political scene. Prime Minister [Horace] Walpole was not in the slightest shaken, although readers ever since have been, as well as delighted and baffled, by this explosion of wit and misanthropy. *Gulliver* is the supreme example of a work of close and detailed political reference, which nevertheless failed as immediate political satire.

## THE DESIGN OF *GULLIVER'S TRAVELS*

When the French translator apologised for omitting several passages not suitable for France, Swift replied:

> If the volumes of Gulliver were designed only for the British Isles, that traveller ought to pass for a very contemptible writer. The same vices and the same follies reign everywhere; at least in the civilized countries of Europe: and the author who writes only for one city, one province, one kingdom or even one age, does not deserve to be read, let alone translated.

The phrase about vices and follies gives us a key to the structure. Book I (Lilliput) is about folly, shown in bad government: the Lilliputians have a few virtues, and are even Utopian at one point. Book II (Brobdingnag) is an exposition of good government: in contrast to the amiable and sensible giants, mankind is seen as petty and vicious. Book III returns to folly: the Laputans have almost entirely lost their wits in the pursuit of scientific speculation. The climax is reached in Book IV: the Houyhnhnms represent virtue, the Yahoos total depravity. They are the poles of behaviour that the human race is capable of attaining.

## POLITICAL ALLEGORY IN THE FIRST TWO BOOKS

Into this framework Swift inserted many detailed references to the England of his day. Book I is a close allegory of the political events of the last years of [British] Queen Anne's reign and the first years of George I's. This allegory is carefully disguised and with good reason. In the 1720s it was dangerous to attack prominent men and especially royalty in too open a manner; with the publication of the *Drapier's Letters* Swift had already risked losing his liberty. Swift sailed as close to the wind as he dared in depicting home politics as a struggle between High Heels and Low Heels, religious controversy as a dispute about the right end to break an egg.

Blefuscu or France supports the Bigendian or Roman Catholic exiles; the heir to the throne has a tendency to High Heels, just as the Prince of Wales favoured the Opposition; Flimnap-Walpole capers along the tightrope of political job-bery. These identifications are obvious, but in the figure of Gulliver there is a deeper allegory. Except for the moment when he puts out the fire, Gulliver is not Swift but Swift's friend [English statesman and writer] Bolingbroke, and sometimes an amalgam of Bolingbroke and [British politi-cian] Harley. The story is taken to 1714, when Bolingbroke was threatened with impeachment for treasonable corre-spondence with the Pretender [James II's son] and fled to France. The point of this interpretation is that Swift was not the complete egoist that some critics have seen in him: rather than expressing his many personal disappointments in a mood of self-pity, he is sending a message of loyalty to his friends in trouble. Brobdingnag is largely a political utopia—England as it might have been if the Tories had re-mained in power. Swift is being realistic here, implying that if Englishmen could not become Houyhnhnms they could at least be like the Brobdingnagians, who though rather repul-sive when you look at them too closely are basically sound in their politics. Swift took politics to be an essential part of the good life, and venerated the memory of his patron Tem-ple, who may be represented in the King of Brobdingnag. The king is also a Tory mouthpiece: among the things he de-nounces, a 'mercenary standing army in the midst of peace, and among a free people' and the national debt, were com-mon objects of Tory attack. But the basis of the Brobdingna-gian state is the humanist principle 'that whoever could make two Ears of Corn, or two Blades of Grass grow upon a Spot of Ground where only one grew before, would deserve better of mankind and do more essential Service to his Country, than the whole Race of Politicians Put together', which is still true today.

## SATIRE IN BOOK III

The third voyage was written last of the four, and is the least effective as satire or imaginative creation. Laputa, the Flying Island, is the court and government of George I, which keeps England and Ireland in subjection. The revolt of Lindalino (Dublin) was an incident so dangerously topical that it was suppressed in the early editions. The Laputans fail to crush this revolt because they are afraid of the combustible fuel directed at the island's adamantine bottom: a direct allegory of Swift's *Drapier's Letters,* by which he had just achieved a victory over the English government. The Laputans are typically English in their love of political intrigue (as Swift wrote to [his friend] Stella from London, 'the rabble here are much more inquisitive in politics than (they are) in Ireland') and in their love of music, a reference to the keen dispute between the supporters of Italian opera and of [German composer George] Handel in the 1720s. The centre-piece of the satire is the Academy of Projectors, which is partly directed at the scientists of the Royal Society and of the Dublin Philosophical Society. It must not be assumed that Swift was completely philistine [ignorant] about science: as we have seen, he admired the practical inventor who could grow two ears of corn where one grew before, which is in accordance with the Baconian [after the philosophy of George Bacon] aims of the Royal Society. He certainly knew more about science than most literary men have done, as is shown by his close parody of scientific papers, based on careful reading of the *Transactions* of the Royal Society. But he considered scientific speculation as secondary to the main business of man upon earth, which is right conduct. There were less worthy reasons for his attitude: he saw the great [scientist Sir Isaac] Newton mainly as a Whig politician who had been called in by the Government for support over 'Wood's Halfpence' [a penny coined by William Wood. In his *Drapier's Letters,* Swift urged the Irish not to take these coins], and he resented the lack of patronage [support] now given to men of letters, as compared with the great days of Queen Anne. Finally 'projector' meant not so much a scientist, for which the usual eighteenth-century word was 'virtuoso' but a promoter of get-rich-quick schemes. Swift is also satirising the speculative financial projects which were floated in large numbers in the six years before 1720, when the greatest of them, the South Sea Bubble [a scheme to pay off the English national debt], burst.

## THE REJECTION OF ALL GOVERNMENTS

Book IV, in which the rational horses appear, is still concerned with politics, although the argument has moved from the particular to the general. Whereas Book II contains a stock Tory attack on standing armies, Swift now offers a gen-

eral indictment of war (chapter 5) in absolute terms. Against
the complacent ideas about colonisation held in his time and
optimistically expressed by [English writer Daniel] Defoe,
Swift opposes his perception of the naked truth (chapter 12) in
his most startling reductive language:

> For instance, a Crew of Pyrates are driven by a Storm they
> know not whither; at length a Boy discovers Land from the
> Top-mast; they go on Shore to rob and plunder; they see an
> harmless People, are entertained with Kindness, they give the
> Country a new Name, they take formal Possession of it for the
> King, they set up a rotten Plank or a Stone for a Memorial,
> they murder two or three Dozen of the Natives, bring away a
> Couple more by Force for a Sample, return home, and get
> their Pardon. Here commences a new Dominion acquired
> with a Title by *Divine Right.* Ships are sent out with the first
> Opportunity; the Natives driven out or destroyed, the Princes
> tortured to discover their Gold; a free Licence given to all Acts
> of Inhumanity and Lust; the Earth reeking with the Blood of
> its Inhabitants; and this execrable Crew of Butchers em-
> ployed in so pious an Expedition, is a modern Colony sent to
> convert and civilize an idolatrous and barbarous People.

Swift has moved from opposition to particular Governments
to the apparently total rejection of all governments; and that
is the doctrine of anarchism. It is striking that the philosophical anarchist [English writer and philosopher] William
Godwin quotes Book IV of *Gulliver's Travels* with approval,
in support of his argument that all political institutions are
totally corrupt; and it is paradoxical that the great Tory
High-churchman should have reached so subversive a position. His vision was one which no one could take seriously
in the eighteenth or nineteenth centuries, but one which finally came true in the [German] concentration camps of [the
Holocaust]. His mistake was to attack the wrong age.

# CHAPTER 2

# Theme and Technique in *Gulliver's Travels*

# The Failure of Language in *Gulliver's Travels*

Brian Tippet

Brian Tippet argues that *Gulliver's Travels* is a book about words themselves, and that language, whether of the Lilliputians, Brobdingnagians, or Houyhnhnms, is weakest when it is most complex and long-winded, and strongest when simplified and short. Tippet argues that Swift's conclusions are: The more words we use, the more we are apt to lie. Truthtelling lies in brevity. This is an ironic stance for a writer to take, but one of Swift's satiric targets is the writing of books. Ultimately *Gulliver's Travels* is a book about Gulliver's writing a book about his travels. Although the fictional Gulliver is writing to a fictional contemporary reader, our understanding of Swift's satire adds a completely new and more profound level of meaning to a book in which language is often the enemy. Brian Tippet has served as dean of academic affairs at King Alfred's College in Winchester, England.

Of all the acquisitions made by mankind in its development none is more wonderful, more curious, more deeply formative of consciousness and yet more likely to be taken for granted than language and the elaborate communicative forms, conventions, techniques and artifacts into which it has evolved. *Gulliver's Travels* bears witness to this in various ways. Languages and language-learning are, for example, one of the essential ingredients of each of the voyages. The ways in which language is used and abused are an important indicator of the intellectual and moral condition of each of the lands Gulliver visits. And our attention is repeatedly drawn, through Gulliver's references to his own book and his own writing, to the strangeness of Swift's chosen way of depicting reality through an extravagant fiction which masquerades as Gulliver's plain truth and indeed, to the strangeness of writing itself.

## THE LANGUAGE OF LILLIPUT

We begin in Lilliput with the impenetrable strangeness of an unknown language with Gulliver the witness to what might just as well be a dumb-show. Cries of 'Hekinah Degul' and 'Tolgo Phonac' are followed by a long speech from a ladder by a Person of Quality, 'whereof I understood not one Syllable'. Gulliver, no mean linguist, tries all the languages he knows—High and Low Dutch, Latin, French, Spanish, Italian, and Lingua Franca—'but all to no purpose'. In a short time, however, he has made great progress in learning the language. We as readers are still at a loss but, now an insider with the confident hold on things that the possession of language gives, he is able to scatter Lilliputian words with familiar ease: *Lumos Kelmin pesso desmar Lon Emposo, Nardac, Drurr, Brundrecal, Glumgluff, Burglum, Glimigrim* (by the Blefuscudians called *Flunec), Snilpall.*

Once he has penetrated the language barrier Gulliver's experiences in Lilliput afford a number of significant reminders of the ways of language in a sophisticated society, chiefly in laudatory references to the King and the chilling legal language of the articles of liberty and the impeachment: 'did maliciously, traitorously, and devilishly, by the discharge of his Urine, put out the said Fire kindled in the said Apartment lying and being within the Precincts of the said Royal Palace'. The next two voyages contain certain other parodies of specialised language: nautical ('we reeft the Foresail and set him, we hawled aft the Foresheet'), scientific ('let AB represent a Line drawn Cross the Dominions of Balnibari; let the Line *c d* represent the Load-stone') and exotic ("My Tongue is in the Mouth of my Friend'). We are in Brobdingnag offered the linguistic ideals of brevity and simplicity and in Laputa perversions of these ideals in the elimination of language by the use of linguistic back-packs, the *reductio ad absurdum* of directness, or in the mystification of the simple as in the misinterpretation of the homely directness of 'Our Brother Tom has just got, the Piles' according to the Anagranimatick Method: 'Resist—a Plot is brought home—The Tour.'

## THE INNOCENT LANGUAGE OF THE HOUYHNHNMS

By contrast the language of the Houyhnhnms takes us back as if to the beginnings of time, reminding us of Adam's naming of things and recalling that stage in linguistic evolution which [Greek historian] Diodorus Siculus describes:

> And though the sounds which they made were at first unintelligible and indistinct, yet gradually they came to give articulation to their speech, and by agreeing with one another upon symbols for each thing which presented itself to them, made known among themselves the significance which was attached to each term. But since groups of this kind arose over every part of the inhabited world, not all men had the same language, inasmuch as every group organised the elements of its speech by mere chance.

If language begins with random sounds to which meanings are then attached, the signs of the process are still apparent in the Houyhnhnms' words which, as readers-aloud know only too well, are variants of the horse's whinny. Semantically too their language is primitive, limited in range and displaying simple patterns of word formation. Inevitably the language has no expressions for things or concepts which have no place in their world. In their state of innocence only 'Yahoo' can supply the term for 'bad' and Gulliver's difficulties in explaining a complicated fallen world are immense: 'Power, Government, War, Law, Punishment, and a Thousand other Things had no Terms, wherein that Language could express them; which made the Difficulty almost insuperable to give my Master any conception of what I meant' (II.iv.291). We are given the circumlocutions [a long way of saying something] to which he has to resort in defining a soldier and a lie, but we are left to imagine the verbal contortions required as he works his way through dizzying accumulations of occupations, crimes, follies and diseases, all of which must be described *ab initio* [from the beginning]: 'Begging, Robbing, Stealing, Cheating, Pimping, Forswearing, Flattering, Suborning, Forging, Gaming, Lying, Fawning, Hectoring, Voting, Scribling, Stargazing, Poysoning, Whoring, Canting, Libelling, Free-thinking, and the like Occupations.' Catalogues such as this are a measure not only of the immensity of Gulliver's explanatory task but also, since language is the mirror of its society, of the extent to which society has deviated from the primal simplicities represented by the world of the Houyhnhnms. A myriad of new vices demands a multitude of new words; unknown vices need no words.

## LANGUAGE AND LIES

The most telling of all the circumlocutions is the phrase for a lie—'the Thing which is not'—which nicely captures a worldview in which falsehood is so illogical as to be nonsensical. Gulliver's master's comments on the subject are important:

> For he argued thus; That the use of Speech was to make us understand one another, and to receive Information on Facts; now if anyone *said the thing which was not*, these ends were defeated; because I cannot properly be said to understand him; and I am so far from receiving Information that he leaves me worse than in ignorance. (IV.iv.286)

In his innocence the Houyhnhnm provides a purely logical model of language; the *Travels* presents a catalogue of examples of deviations from this ideal. The corruption of the world manifests itself in the corruption of language which departs from its primal function of truth-telling. There are, for example, the extravagant falsehoods of the conventional tributes to the four-inch King of Lilliput: 'Delight and Terror of the Universe: Taller than the Sons of Men; whose Feet press down to the Center, and whose Head strikes against the Sun.' There are the declarations of the King's lenity which no one believes and everyone fears. The scientists of Brobdingnag, called upon to examine Gulliver, believe they have given a modern scientific explanation whereas they have merely provided a clever new term which advances knowledge not at all. Among politicians, lawyers and historians a law of contraries operates: thus a chief minister 'applies his Mind to all Uses, except the Indication of his Mind; . . . he never tells a Truth, but with an Intent that you should take it for a Lye; nor a Lye, but with Design that you should take it for a Truth'. In Glubbdubdrib Gulliver learns of the misrepresentations of the historians: 'I found the World had been misled by prostitute Writers, to ascribe the greatest Exploits in War to Cowards, the Wisest Council to Fools.' And the lawyers 'prove by Words multiplied from this Purpose, that *White* is *Black*, and *Black* is *White*'.

## MORE WORDS EQUALS MORE LIES

This last example makes two connections explicit: that in Swift's satiric vision the multiplying of words is inseparable from falsehood and that language follows the general 'multi-

plying' tendencies of the fallen world in its departure from
primal simplicities. It is significant that abuses and abusers of
language should figure so prominently in Gulliver's catalogues of villainy in Voyage IV. The vicious 'occupations' listed
in Chapter 6 include forswearing, flattering, lying, hectoring,
scribbling, canting and libelling; and in Chapter 10 the satirical indictment is drawn not only against such as Highwaymen, Bawds, Gamesters and Politicians but also informers
who watch words and actions or forge accusations for hire,
gibers, censurers, backbiters, controvertists and tedious talk-
ers. By contrast, in the conversations of the Houyhnhnms
'nothing passed but what was useful, expressed in the fewest
and most significant Words' and 'there was no Tediousness,
Heat, or Difference of Sentiments'. This is not an entirely remote ideal, for the Brobdingnagians cultivate a style which is
'clear, masculine, and smooth, but not Florid; for they avoid
nothing more than multiplying unnecessary words, or using
various Expressions.' And in that country no law may exceed
twenty-two words 'expressed in the most plain and simple
Terms' which offer no scope for conflicting interpretations.

## A SATIRE ON BOOKS

What makes the Brobdingnagians exceptional is that, while
having all the communicative resources of a modern civilisa-
tion, they use these with rational restraint so that they do not
lose their hold on essentials in a flood of falsifying words. The
oral, preliterate culture of the Houyhnhnms is safe in its time-
warp from the malign consequences of the Gutenberg revolution whereas the Brobdingnagians, older and wiser in these
matters than the European countries, have come to a rational
accommodation with the printed word. 'They have had the Art
of Printing, as well as the *Chinese*, Time out of Mind. But their
Libraries are not very large; for that of the King's, which is
reckoned the largest, doth not amount to above a thousand
volumes.' Elsewhere in the world the multiplication of words
is accelerated by means of the press. Thus Gulliver speaks of
"Pyramids of Law-Books', *hundreds* of commentators on
Homer and Aristotle shamefacedly avoiding their 'Principals',
*hundreds* of books on the egg controversy in Lilliput, and
*thousands* of books on the art of government. With appropriate irony the *Travels* itself fuels the same tendency, prompting
tribes of 'Answerers, Considerers, Observers, Reflectors, De-
tectors, Remarkers' to rush into print. And the Lagadan writ-

ing machine (whereby 'the most ignorant Person at a reasonable charge, and with a little bodily Labour, may write Books in Philosophy, Poetry, Politicks, Law, Mathematics and Theology, with the least Assistance from Genius or Study') gives us a futuristic glimpse of mechanisation accelerating and depersonalising the process. We can detect in all this a number of contemporary influences and concerns. The writing machine is quite evidently a satirical glance at the experiments with mechanical writing conducted by John Wilkins of the Royal Society. The concern that printing has opened the floodgates was shared by [English poet Alexander] Pope who, writing in an ironical vein about himself and his poem *The Dunciad*, said: 'He lived in those days, when (after providence had permitted the Invention of Printing as a scourge for the Sins of the learned) Paper also became so cheap, and printers so numerous, that a deluge of authors cover'd the land.'. . .

Although on several occasions Gulliver draws attention to his own reading, only one of the books he reads is described at any length. It is the 'little old treatise' which he finds in Glumdalclitch's bed chamber, a work of popular morality 'in little esteem except among Women and the Vulgar', which 'treats of the weakness of human kind'.

> This Writer went through all the usual Topicks of *European* Moralists; shewing how diminutive, contemptible, and helpless an Animal was Man in his own Nature; how unable to defend himself from the Inclemencies of the Air, or the Fury of wild Beasts: How much he was excelled by one Creature in Strength, by another in Speed, by a third in Foresight, by a fourth in Industry. He added, that Nature was degenerated in these latter declining Ages of the World, and could now produce only small abortive Births by Comparison of those in ancient times. He said, it was very reasonable to think there must have been Giants in former Ages. . . . From this Way of Reasoning the Author drew several more Applications useful in the Conduct of life, but needless here to repeat. For my own Part, I could not avoid reflecting, how universally this Talent was spread of drawing Lectures in Morality, or indeed rather Matters of Discontent and repining, from the Quarrels we raise with Nature. (II.vii.178)

On the face of it Gulliver's dismissal is so well-grounded and so tellingly formulated that it might seem to carry Swift's endorsement and to demand our consent. The little old book's themes were indeed commonplace ones in seventeenth-century moral discourses and perhaps therefore Swift is ridiculing arguments, in themselves questionable, which had become stale with repetition. But unsophisticated readers are, in Swift, more likely to have their priorities right than the learned and consciously clever and 'moral Applications useful in the Conduct of life' are not lightly to be set aside. What is even more curious is that the book's argument bears a close resemblance to some of the major themes of the *Travels*. Have we here discovered the book we are reading contained within itself? 'How diminutive contemptible and helpless an Animal was Man in his own Nature' aptly enough describes a central theme of the first two voyages and foreshadows the emphasis upon human insufficiency in the fourth. Far from being the sole prerogative of tedious moralists, reflections of this kind are given memorable expression by [French essayist, Michel de] Montaigne. His *Apology for Raymond de Sebonde,* which scholars have regarded as one of Swift's influences, emphasises the helplessness of man in ways which recall the fourth voyage: 'we are the only animal abandoned, naked upon the bare earth . . . nor having wherewithal to arm and clothe us, but by the spoil of others'. Thus the little old treatise, a book within a book, is an imperfect mirror *and* a critique of the book which contains it. This may serve as a warning that we should not reduce *Gulliver's Travels* to a restatement of familiar pessimistic themes. In a world in which reason is problematical, 'where men can argue with Plausibility on both Sides of a Question', interpretation cannot be as simple as that.

Within this book's fictional world, the historical sequence which runs from the evolution of spoken language through the development of writing to the invention of printing and the proliferation of writers, readers and books, comes to its conclusion with Gulliver writing, Motte publishing, the gentle Reader reading and the first Answerers answering *Travels into Several Remote Nations of the World* (though we Answerers are still at it). The *Travels* does not stand aloof from the world it portrays: it is implicated in it and is itself a prime example of what it satirises. This self-referential tendency is no surprise for we have another example of the same thing in Gulliver's final stance as a man smitten with pride castigating men smitten with pride.

## A BOOK THAT REFERS TO ITSELF

In the first place *Gulliver's Travels* draws attention to itself as a particular kind of publication. The book's typography, title page, maps and diagrams immediately identify it with contemporary books of travel, one of the largest and most popular categories of publication. The references in the introductory sections to the text's composition, transmission and reception (the style corrected, the book pruned of nautical details and politically dangerous passages, the manuscript delivered anonymously at night) together with Gulliver's irritable complaints about omissions, mistaken times and dates and the misspelling 'Brobdingnag', all help to give the book its air of authenticity but also exemplify the fact that in the modern world communication is attended by innumerable complications and corruptions. And in carrying promises of supplementary works and in provoking written responses the *Travels* not only sounds authentically contemporary but is seen to occasion the kind of proliferation the book appears to condemn.

Authorial business of this kind makes an important contribution to our sense of Gulliver as a character. As [critic Everett] Zimmerman has remarked, what we observe in reading the *Travels* is not simply a man going through certain adventures but a man writing a book about them. Gulliver's authorial habits are borrowed from his real-life counterpart, Captain William Dampier [English explorer and sea captain], and while taking pleasure in the skill of the impersonation we also realise that in imitating Dampier Gulliver becomes an agent and advocate of the new science. His plain style, his omnivorous curiosity, his attention to observational detail are the hallmarks of a traveller who is acting, like Dampier, under the Royal Society's instructions to voyagers. And thus, as he does in *A Modest Proposal* and *A Tale of a Tub*, Swift adopts a standpoint and a voice to which he himself is antipathetic. As an acolyte of the Royal Society, Gulliver's most persistent claim is to truthfulness. He is irritated by those who 'are so bold as to think my Book of Travels a meer Fiction out of mine own Brain' and who 'have gone so far as to drop Hints, that the *Houyhnhnms* and *Yahoos* have no more Existence than the Inhabitants of Utopia'. And if we should find him a trifle dull, this is because he is no mere entertainer:

> I could perhaps like others have astonished thee with strange improbable Tales; but I rather chose to relate plain Matter of Fact in the simplest Manner and Style; because my principal Design was to inform, and not to amuse thee.

In one sense this is a typical piece of ironical topsyturvydom: that in giving us giants and midgets, a flying island, people who do not die, man-apes and talking horses Gulliver should have the effrontery to claim kinship with the writers of scientific travel books and behave as if superior to those mere entertainers who deal in improbable oddities and wonders. At the same time, however, we may reflect that in reading the *Travels* we are continually colliding with some extremely uncomfortable matters of fact about our world—its grossness, extravagancies and injustices, its falsehoods, follies and cruelties. On the surface there is an entertaining period piece, a transaction in the manner of Grub Street [the world of impoverished writers and literary hacks], between Lemuel Gulliver and an imaginary reading public, in the person of the 'gentle Reader', which belongs to the book's fiction; but secreted within is a transaction between Swift and ourselves, a transaction which restores strangeness to all kinds of things—and these include even the act of reading and responding to his words.

# The Frailty of Human Beings in *Gulliver's Travels*

Paul Fussell

While eighteenth century humanists celebrated the abilities and accomplishments of humans, they were also keenly aware of people's limitations. According to noted critic Paul Fussell, this theme is clearly manifested in Gulliver's frailty during his travels. Swift's hero is put through physical travails that are at least the equivalent of his mental and emotional tests. In this excerpt from *The Rhetorical World of Augustan Humanism,* Fussell details the astounding number of injuries Gulliver suffers during his travels. Thus Swift suggests that mankind's high self-image is not enough to save him from the inherent weaknesses of his mind and body. Paul Fussell has taught at The University of Pennsylvania. His many books include *Poetic Meter and Poetic Form, The Great War and Modern Memory* and *Ethics and Imagery from Swift to Burke.*

The theme of human limitations is admirably 'incorporated' by Swift in the image of the frailty of Gulliver's body. Indeed, it is remarkable what happens physically to poor Gulliver during his four voyages. He does far more suffering than acting. Even though as a surgeon he is more likely than most to dwell obsessively on his own physical injuries, and e' though his commitment to the ideals of the Royal Soc [English scientific academy] impels him to deliver his n ar rative with a comically detailed circumstantiality, he records a really startling number of hurts. In the voyage to Lilliput, for example, his hair is painfully pulled, and his hands and face are blistered by needle-like arrows. During his stay among the people of Brobdingnag he is battered so

badly that he appears almost accident-prone: his flesh is
punctured by wheat-beards; twice his sides are painfully
crushed; he is shaken up and bruised in a box; his nose and
forehead are grievously stung by flies as big as larks; he suffers painful contusions from a shower of gigantic hailstones;
he 'breaks' his shin on a snailshell; and he is pummelled
about the head and body by a linnet's wings. And during his
fourth voyage he is brought again into dire physical jeop-
ardy: his final series of physical ordeals begins as his hand
is painfully squeezed by a horse. Finally, as he leaves Houyhnhnmland, Swift contrives that Gulliver shall suffer a
wholly gratuitous arrow wound on the inside of his left knee
('I shall carry the Mark to my Grave'). Looking back on the
whole extent of Gulliver's experiences before his final return
to England, we are hardly surprised that his intellectuals at
the end have come unhinged: for years his body has been
beaten, dropped, squeezed, lacerated, and punctured. When
all is said, the experiences which transform him from a
fairly bright young surgeon into a raging megalomaniac
have been almost as largely physical as intellectual and psychological. So powerfully does Swift reveal Gulliver's purely
mental difficulties at the end of the fourth voyage that we
may tend to forget that Gulliver has also been made to un-
dergo the sorest physical trials. During the four voyages he
has been hurt so badly that, although he is normally a taci-
turn, unemotional, 'Roman' sort of person, he has been reduced to weeping three times; so severely has he been in-
jured at various times that at least twenty-four of his total
travelling days he has spent recuperating in bed.

## GULLIVER'S NARROW ESCAPES

In addition to these actual injuries which Gulliver endures,
he also experiences a number of narrow escapes, potential
injuries, and pathetic fears of physical hurt. In Lilliput the
vulnerability of his eyes is insisted upon: an arrow barely
misses his left eye, and only his spectacles prevent the loss
of both his eyes as he works to capture the Blefuscan fleet.
Furthermore, one of the Lilliputian punishments decreed for
Quinbus Flestrin is that his eyes be put out. And during the
Brobdingnagian trip Gulliver's experience is one of an almost continuous narrow escape from serious injury. He almost falls from the hand of the farmer and off the edge of the
table. Stumbling over a crust, he falls flat on his face and

barely escapes injury. After being held in a child's mouth, he is dropped, and he is saved only by being miraculously caught in a woman's apron. He is tossed into a bowl of cream, knocked down but not badly hurt by a shower of falling apples, and clutched dangerously between a spaniel's teeth. He is lucky to escape serious injury during a nasty tumble into a mole hill, whereupon he 'coined some Lye not worth remembering, to excuse my self for spoiling my Cloaths'. And during the sojourn at Laputa, he is afraid of some 'hurt' befalling him in his encounter with the magician.

## OTHERS ARE ALSO HARMED

But Gulliver, who acts like a sort of physically vulnerable *Ur*-Boswell [a recorder of other's deeds, after British Diarist James Boswell] on the Grand Tour, is not the only one in the book who suffers or who fears injury: the creatures he is thrown among also endure catastrophes of pain and damage, often curiously particularized by Swift. Thus in Lilliput, two or three of the rope-dancers break their limbs in falls. A horse, slipping part way through Gulliver's handkerchief, strains a shoulder. The grandfather of the Lilliputian monarch, it is reported, as a result of breaking his egg upon the larger end suffered a cut finger. In the same way, the fourth voyage seems busy with apparently gratuitous details of injury and pain: for example, Gulliver carefully tells us that an elderly Houyhnhnm 'of Quality' alighted from his Yahoo-drawn sledge 'with his Hind-feet forward, having by Accident got a Hurt in his Left Forefoot'.

## CLOTHING AS METAPHOR

Nor are all the manifold injuries in *Gulliver's Travels* confined to the bodies of Gulliver and his hosts. Gulliver's clothing and personal property suffer constant damage, and when they are not actually being damaged, Gulliver is worrying that at any moment they may be hurt. We are not surprised that a shipwrecked mariner suffers damage to his clothing and personal effects, but we are surprised that Gulliver constantly goes out of his way to call attention to the damages and losses he suffers: his scimitar, his hat, his breeches—all are damaged in Lilliput, and the damage is punctiliously recounted. In Brobdingnag the familiar process of damage and deterioration begins all over again: a fall into a bowl of milk utterly spoils Gulliver's suit; his

stockings and breeches are soiled when he is thrust into a
marrow bone; and his suit—what's left of it—is further
ruined by being daubed with frog slime and 'bemired' with
cow dung. In the third voyage our attention is invited to the
fact that his hat has again worn out, and in the fourth voyage
we are told yet again by Gulliver that his clothes are 'in a de-
clining Condition'.

Gulliver's clothes and personal effects, in fact, at times
seem to be Gulliver himself: this is the apparent state of
things which fascinates the Houyhnhnm before whom Gulliver undresses; and this ironic suggestion of an equation between Gulliver and his clothing, reminding us of the ironic
'clothes philosophy' of Section II of *A Tale of a Tub*, Swift exploits to suggest that damage to Gulliver's frail garments is
the equivalent of damage to the frail Gulliver. The vulnerability of Gulliver's clothing, that is, is a symbol three degrees
removed from what it appears to signify: damage to the
clothes is symbolic of damage to the body; and damage to
the body is symbolic of damage to Gulliver's complacent
self-esteem.

## MAN'S PATHETIC FRAGILITY

These little incidents of injury and destruction are pervasive
in *Gulliver's Travels*, as we are reminded by the recurrence—
very striking once we are attuned to it—of words like 'hurt',
'injury', 'damage', 'accident', 'mischief', 'misfortune', and
'spoiled'. When we focus on what is happening physically in
*Gulliver's Travels*, we sense the oblique presence of this motif of frailty and vulnerability even in passages which really
address themselves to something quite different. For example: 'His Majesty [the Emperor of Blefuscu] presented me . . .
with his Picture at full length, which I immediately put into
one of my Gloves, to keep it from being hurt.' It is as if Swift
were determined not to let us forget that there is a pathetic
fragility in all his fictional objects, whether animate or in-
animate.

And Swift seems to have provided within his text a key to
these pervasive reminders of the vulnerability of man and
the fragility of his personal effects. In the second voyage, we
are told in a voice which sounds perhaps more Swiftian than
Gulliverian of a 'little old Treatise' treasured now only by elderly women and the more credulous vulgar, a copy of
which Glumdalclitch has been given by her governess. The

burden of this mysterious little book, we are told, is precisely the theme of the physical frailty of man: the book shows 'how diminutive, contemptible, and helpless an Animal . . . [is] Man in his own Nature'. Like [English writer Samuel] Johnson's version of [Roman poet] Juvenal in *London*, the book emphasizes man's liability to accident and injury; it argues that 'the very Laws of Nature absolutely required we should have been made in the Beginning, of a Size more large and robust, not so liable to Destruction from every little Accident of a Tile falling from an House, or a Stone cast from the Hand of a Boy, or of being drowned in a little Brook.' Here Swift appears to avail himself of the myth of the Decay of Nature as a fictional surrogate for the Christian myth of the Fall. Although, as [noted Swift critic] Miss Kathleen Williams reminds us, Godfrey Goodman's *The Fall of Man, or the Corruption of Nature* (1616) is perhaps the kind of 'little old Treatise' Swift has in mind, I think we shall not go far wrong if we associate—even though we do not identify—Glumdalclitch's conservative little book with the Bible itself. The theme that Swift realizes by means of the image of Gulliver's physical frailty appears quintessentially humanistic: the theme is the inadequacy of an unassisted self-esteem in redeeming man from his essential frailties of mind and spirit. . . . In one of its most significant moods the Augustan humanist mind conceives of man thus as a little delicate cage of bones and skin constantly at the mercy of accidental damage or destruction.

# Gulliver Is an Unreliable Narrator

Karen Lawrence, Betsy Seifter, and Lois Ratner

In Gulliver, Swift creates a flat, precise, mostly non-judgmental narrator who often tells us events in painstakingly deliberate fashion. The effect of this realistic narrative is, paradoxically, to make the reader question the reliability of Gulliver's reporting. In obsessively adhering to the details of the journey, Gulliver misses the larger implications of his story. In each part, what Gulliver reports must be filtered through Swift's satiric purposes to get to the real meaning of *Gulliver's Travels.* Karen Lawrence has taught at the University of Utah. She is the author of *Penelope Voyages: Women and Travel in the British Literary Tradition* and other books on travel literature. Betsy Seifter and Lois Ratner hold advanced degrees from Columbia University. Ratner is the author of *Harmony: Structure and Style.*

The factual style is Gulliver's characteristic narrative mode, and the flat, literal-minded reporting establishes his persona: he is fastidious, precise, gullible, and so compulsively comprehensive that he seems incapable of editing or evaluating the data he is scrupulously recording. We hear about everything, from the exact height of the trees in Lilliput, to the number of inhabitants of Lorbrulgrud in Brobdingnag, to his inventive methods of performing bodily functions. Of course, Gulliver is not merely, or solely, a neutral reporter. He has opinions too, for example, his contempt for the treasurer of Lilliput (I, vi, meaning Book I, Chapter vi) or his disapproval of the Brobdingnagian king for refusing to learn the secrets of gunpowder (II, vii); but apart from momentary lapses into emotion and bias, he is primarily obsessed with "facts," what he can measure and describe.

## GULLIVER AS UNRELIABLE NARRATOR

One of the effects of the welter of description and quantification is, curiously, to render Gulliver's account suspect. Under the guise of extreme fidelity to the "truth" he is quintessentially unreliable, a naive witness to scenes and events whose import almost uniformly escapes him. The suppression of judgment and reflection in favor of record keeping creates an ironic doubleness, for there is a vast discrepancy between the overt story Gulliver tells and the underlying implications of that story.

## STRANGENESS OF GULLIVER'S NARRATION

The reader is directed toward those implications by the strangeness of the narration, its exaggerated completeness and its crucial omissions. In part the preoccupation with quantifiable phenomena and observed facts constitutes a parody of travel literature, with its cataloguing of exotic sights and unusual experiences. Such literature tells the reader both more and less than he wants to know. Gulliver's own references to travel literature reinforce the satiric emphasis on the amassing of circumstantial detail, as well as on the omnivorous self that does the amassing. For example, at the end of Book II, Chapter i, Gulliver's comments on his motives for writing (his concern for the public benefit and his interest in truth) and his compunctions about becoming "tedious and trifling" delineate him as a self-centered, self-conscious traveler who jots down his every action and opinion ostensibly for the greater good of humanity. Such a remark also serves to disarm criticism as Gulliver proceeds to belabor all his points at length, taxing the reader's patience and committing various assaults on decorum.

Thus, Gulliver tells us what he ate (the meals of 1728 Lilliputians per day), where he slept (the baby's cradle in Brobdingnag), whom he met (the *struldbruggs* of Laputa), and how he communicated (in snippets of foreign languages, of which he offers samples). But he never makes explicit the value or meaning of his experiences—that is, what these races and places signify—except in the case of Houyhnhnmland, where the extremity of his praise has the same suspect ring as the neutrality of his reports from the other lands. Like many a traveler before and since, Gulliver has the experience but misses the meaning, a meaning which Swift forces the reader to supply.

## A SYMBOLIC STORY

One of the ways in which Swift enforces an allegorical reading of the text is by the overt clash between fact and fiction. The realistic references begin to seem surreal, attached as they are to such fantastic subjects as pygmies, giants, mad

### GULLIVER IS NOT JONATHAN SWIFT

*Those who see Jonathan Swift as a madman often make the mistake of confusing the author with his protagonist.*

The first character to demand our attention is Gulliver himself. He is the narrator, the principal actor. We see through his eyes, feel his feelings, share his thoughts. We are in his company from first to last, and it is important that we come to know him as quickly as possible. What is he like and what is his role in the book? He is first of all a bit of a bore, for his mind is irritatingly circumstantial and unimaginative: observe the numerous insignificant biographical details which he gives us in the first pages of the book. Gradually, however, we come to like him and to enjoy his company. In all respects he is an average good man. He has had some university education both at Cambridge and at Leyden, where he studied medicine. He is observant (and we eventually come to be grateful for his gift of close observation and circumstantial reporting, once he has something worth observing and reporting), reasonably intelligent, thoroughly capable in an emergency, and both brave and hopeful. If he lacks imagination and inventiveness, so much the better; for we can be sure that what he tells us, no matter how strange, is true. He is simple, direct, uncomplicated. At the outset he is full of naive good will, and, though he grows less naive and more critical as a result of his voyaging among remote nations, he retains his benevolence throughout the first three voyages. It is a pity that so fine an example of the bluff, good-natured, honest Englishman should at last grow sick and morbid and should be driven mad—but that, I am afraid, is what befalls him.

All of this Gulliver is; but let us notice carefully what he is NOT. He is NOT Jonathan Swift. The meaning of the book is wholly distorted if we identify the Gulliver of the last voyage with his creator, and lay Gulliver's misanthropy at Swift's door. He is a fully rendered, objective, dramatic character.

Samuel H. Monk, "The Pride of Lemuel Gulliver," *Sewanee Review.* Vol. LXIII, 1955, pp. 318–19.

scientists, and philosopher-horses. As in a surrealistic painting, surface appearances and circumstantial details clash bizarrely with the basically dreamlike landscape. For example, the discussion of the dust-licking ceremony before the king of Luggnagg (III, ix) is rendered in a generally neutral expository style, including such details as a description of the poison strewn as a means of executing enemies ("a certain brown powder, of a deadly composition, which being licked up infallibly kills him in twenty-four hours") and an account of an accidental murder when the page forgets to order that the floor be cleansed after a preceding execution ("by which neglect a young lord of great hopes coming to an audience, was unfortunately poisoned, although the king at that time had no design against his life"). The deadpan reporting and the suppression of all judgment on a ritual both absurdly fantastic and morally repugnant recall the style of Swift's "modest proposer, [in his famous satirical essay *A Modest Proposal*]" although Gulliver sounds more like a newspaper reporter than a public official. In both cases, however, there is a surrealistic gap between rhetorical form (ethical persuasion in *A Modest Proposal*, eyewitness account in *Gulliver's Travels*) and content. The reader cannot accept the Luggnagg account at face value and so begins to supply his own subtext on the vanity and treachery of absolute monarchs.

In general, the important facts of *Gulliver's Travels* are the ones that newspaper reporting and travelogue cannot accommodate. What comes through Gulliver's neutral style is that the Lilliputians are contemptibly small and the Brobdingnagians impressively, if grotesquely, big in comparison with himself; that the projectors of Laputa are lunatics and the horses of Houyhnhnmland egomaniacs. Confining himself to "certifiable" data, Gulliver gives us their measurements but not their measure.

In a sense, then, the realistic style determines the whole nature of the narrative: it establishes Gulliver as a limited, excessively naive observer, and creates the effect of discrepancy which is the basis for the satire.

# Swift's Technique of Reducing Men to Machines Enhances the Satire

John M. Bullitt

According to John M. Bullitt, one of Swift's techniques is to reduce thinking processes to mechanical ones, and therefore satirize the way in which people arrive at ideas. In Part I, for example, the Lilliputians are often little better than mechanical puppets, and the satire arises from the gap between their lofty pretensions and their diminutive size. Here the true object of Swift's satire is not the Lilliputians but human beings, who are forced to equate themselves with the tiny people. In Part II, Gulliver himself assumes the role of the mechanical puppet who appears foolish as he attempts to impress his gargantuan hosts. John M. Bullitt has taught at Harvard University. He is the author of *Jonathan Swift and the Anatomy of Satire*, from which this selection is taken, and the co-editor of *The Yale Edition of the Works of Samuel Johnson*.

Of the many ways in which men's awareness is misdirected from what is essential to what is nonessential, the false emphasis upon the artifice of methods and schemes is, in Swift's satire, among the most prominent. Both directly and obliquely through parody, logic, and allegory, Swift reduces the substitution of art for nature to the ridiculous and contemptible. The inflexibility and blind precipitance of method and artifice when separated from the natural ends to which they should work may be readily seen to resemble the mechanical efficiency and unawareness of a machine. It is not surprising, therefore, to find that [French philosopher Henri] Bergson defined the "very quintessence of pedantry [paying undo attention to rules]" as "nothing else than art pretending to outdo nature." A similar distinction between natural process and the artificial creation of man's brain is made by Swift as the basic premise in [Swift's essay] *The Mechanical Operation of the Spirit* for ridiculing the enthusiasm of fanatic preachers:

> . . . I desire the curious Reader to distinguish, First between an Effect grown from *Art* into *Nature,* and one that is natural from its Beginning; Secondly, between an Effect wholly natural, and one which has only a natural Foundation, but where the Superstructure is entirely Artificial. For, the first and last of these, I understand to come within the Districts of my Subject.

The trenchancy and humour of this satire derives largely from Swift's remarkable talent for reducing an intellectual concept to a physical and mechanical operation. . . .

## THE COMEDY OF MECHANISM

The use of the mechanical symbol . . . characterizes the . . . satire in *Gulliver's Travels.* Particularly is this true in the first two voyages. In "A Voyage to Lilliput" the very diminutiveness of the Lilliputians in relation to Gulliver creates the sense of their being tiny, mechanical toys, imitating the gestures of men but without, so to speak, man's soul. Certainly this suggestion of automatism [mechanical movements] has contributed to the perennial popularity among children of the *Travels;* it probably is also a cause, among adult and more critical readers, of the feeling that the Lilliputians are better vehicles for comic satire than for *directly* expressing moral ideals. At least, chapter six, which details the noble and "original institutions" before the "degenerate nature of man" had produced "scandalous corruptions," comes upon us with less of a fine suddenness than do the chapters with a critical and satiric intent. With the exception of that chapter, much of the satire of the voyage arises largely from the disparity between the Lilliputians' vain affectation of human grandeur and the reality of their littleness. And Swift dramatizes the externality of their imitations of humanity by continual reference to their physical gestures and movements. For example, he describes the Lilliputian king standing before the figure of Gulliver: "He held his sword drawn in his hand, to defend himself, if I should happen to break loose; it was almost three inches long, the hilt and the scabbard were gold enriched with diamonds.". . .

The king's gesture is, obviously, a hollow and ineffectual motion when directed against the giant Gulliver; and, as his posture is neither "hateful" nor "detestable," but a diminutive physical imitation of a dangerous gesture, we laugh and contemn without terror or bitterness. The king who thinks himself the "delight and terror of the universe ... whose feet press down to the centre, and whose head strikes against the sun . . ." is ridiculous in proportion to his mechanical imitation of the external forms of humanity without possessing the real power and dangerousness of men. . . . While Gulliver remained on the beach in the bonds of his tiny captors he is addressed by a man of rank who "seemed to be somewhat longer than my middle finger": "He acted every part of an orator, and I could observe many periods of threatenings, and others of promises, pity and kindness.". . . When, . . . we recall that Gulliver at that time had no command of the language and must have determined the oratorical purpose of the Lilliputian entirely by his movements of face and hands, the technique of ridicule is seen to come close to that of the man who understood that jests were being spoken because of his companion's laughing and often speaking. But here the object of the satire is the orator rather than Gulliver. The standardized positioning of an official who is mechanically pursuing the fixed and established forms of behaviour is ludicrous in the same way that the postures assumed in artificial wit are ludicrous. The comedy in Swift's satire against vanity arises from a perception more acute than the simple juxtaposition of big men and little men. The diminutive size of the Lilliputians is used by Swift as a concrete visual aid towards exciting in the reader a strong sense of the comedy of mechanism.

## MEN AS PUPPETS

Needless to say, the satiric objective of Swift in Gulliver's first voyage is to force men to equate themselves with Lilliputians—to make them aware of their own puppetlike appearance of power in contrast to the reality of their weakness. The device of dramatizing the physical gesture as a means to suggest men's intellectual automatism is clearly seen in Swift's satire upon religious schism and political climbing. In the two scenes in which Swift describes the Lilliputian method of gaining court preferment and their dissensions over the High Heels and Low Heels, Swift employs the kind of allegorical technique peculiar to himself. He establishes a correspondence between his own intellectual, pejorative judgment of an idea or situation and a mechanical or physical gesture. Thus, Swift's contempt for the misdirected methods of gaining court favour (by flattery, verbal dexterity, and the like, instead of moral integrity or political acumen) is translated into a series of physical methods (cutting capers on a tightrope and leaping over a stick). Swift enforces the pictorial clarity of this courtly puppetshow by describing an incident, with a possibly particular allegorical application, in which Flimnap is preserved from a nearly fatal accident by the lucky interposition of a pillow. . . . Similarly, Swift's description of the squabbling between religious and political factions as consisting of the difference between High Heels and Low Heels, and the breaking of an egg at the proper end, also reduces Swift's conception of the absurdity of faction to a concrete level of mechanism. The extent to which this technique is successful in reducing intellectual activity to the level of physical automatism is apparent in Swift's brilliant description of the heir to the throne: "We apprehend his Imperial Highness, the Heir to the Crown, to have some tendency towards the High-Heels; at least we can plainly discover one of his heels higher than the other, which gives him a hobble in his gait."

## GULLIVER AS MECHANICAL MAN

The "gay contempt" toward the Lilliputians which Swift arouses by stressing the automatism of their personal movements and gestures is closely paralleled by a similar reduction of Gulliver himself to the likeness of a mechanical toy in *A Voyage to Brobdingnag*. The absurd posture of defense assumed by the Lilliputian king, for example, finds almost a carbon copy in Gulliver's own pretentious manner in the company of his gigantic master: "I drew out my hanger, and flourished with it after the manner of fencers in England. My nurse gave me part of a straw, which I exercised as a pike, having learned the art in my youth." This emphasis upon the empty physical gesture is also the motivating force behind Gulliver's laughter at the thought of the posturing vanity of the English nobility:

> . . . if I had then beheld a company of English lords and ladies in their finery and birth-day clothes, acting their several parts in the most courtly manner, of strutting, and bowing, and prating; to say the truth, I should have been strongly tempted to laugh as much at them as the King and his grandees did at me.

In emphasizing Swift's technique of representing first the Lilliputians and then Gulliver as tiny mechanisms which imitate the external gesture and movements of men, I by no means intend to suggest that this technique alone "explains" either the criticism or the comedy in the first two books of *Gulliver's Travels.* On the contrary, this technique is only one of many which fuse into a totality of comic satire. The comic potential, however, summarized in the Brobdingnagian king's thought of Gulliver as being a "piece of clock-work . . . contrived by some ingenious artist," has been generally overlooked by Swift's commentators. The seriousness of this critical omission is, it seems to me, augmented by two considerations. In the first place, it is clear that the perception of man as a mechanism is one fundamental source of comedy; by incorporating this comic perception into the framework of criticism, therefore, Swift's satire, although often particular in intent, succeeds in its appeal to a general and universal cause of laughter.

# Gulliver's Travels Parodies First-Person Memoirs

J. Paul Hunter

While many critics refuse to consider *Gulliver's Travels* a parody of other works, J. Paul Hunter argues that the book parodies Daniel Defoe's *Robinson Crusoe* directly, and, indirectly, the emerging genre of first-person narrative that led, in the eighteenth century, to the development of the novel. Hunter cites in particular the ludicrous assortment of items with which Gulliver's pockets are stuffed when he arrives in Lilliput. This catalogue of items calls attention to a famous mistake in *Robinson Crusoe*, and also suggests how first-person narratives tend to be artificially constructed fictions rather than realities, because the difficulty of getting all of the facts correct is often insurmountable. J. Paul Hunter has taught at The University of Chicago and served as Dean of Arts and Sciences at The University of Rochester. His books include *Before Novels: Cultural Contexts of Eighteenth-Century English Fiction* and *The Reluctant Pilgrim: Defoe's Emblematic Method and Quest for Form in Robinson Crusoe.* He is also the editor of *The Norton Introduction to Poetry* and *The Norton Critical Edition of Frankenstein.*

*Gulliver's Travels* has generally resisted efforts to consider it parodic [imitating another author's style for comic effect], and some Swift critics lurch toward apoplexy when the very idea of parody is broached within reaching distance of *Gulliver's Travels.* And yet Swift's consciousness of contemporary writing is nearly as apparent there as in [his prose work] *A Tale of a Tub,* and if passages that specifically echo another writer . . .

Excerpted from "Gulliver's Travels and the Novel," by J. Paul Hunter, in *The Genres of "Gulliver's Travels,"* edited by Frederik N. Smith. Copyright © 1990 by Associated University Presses, Inc. Reprinted with the permission of Associated University Presses.

are rare, a large awareness of contemporary writing habits and the prevailing tastes of readers is visible at nearly every turn. Swift's awareness of contemporary travel writers— William Dampier, for example—has been often remarked, and much of the fun in the book's first appearance had to do with its solemn title page: *Travels into Several Remote Nations of the World,* it advertised, promising something quite other than what is delivered. Swift, in one of his letters, has something of a lark in imagining literal-minded readers who are gulled by such an expectation: he speaks of an Irish bishop who, after reading *Gulliver's Travels,* concluded that it was "full of improbable lies, and for his part, he hardly believed a word of it."

But quite beyond its evocation of travel literature, *Gulliver's Travels* engages a whole tradition of fiction that was then in the process of developing, and Swift saw that this new kind of writing was beginning to codify a "modern," significantly new way of perceiving the world. Contemporary narratives of personal experience—scandalous memoirs and chronicles of personal and public political intrigue, as well as books that charted personal travel to far-off places or new experiences— were increasingly sought by a public that wanted material, intellectual, and psychological satisfaction in the conquest of space and the accrual of experience. Because of its new popularity, this subjective writing, whether genuine or fictional, seems to offer a personal yet universal key to reality and, . . . can only deliver on its promise by exaggerated and distorted emblematicism and by verbal sleight-of-hand. . . .

## GULLIVER'S POCKETS

Because Swift's parody works through an accretion and absorption of particulars, it is difficult to illustrate his method without a detailed consideration of the text and its contexts, but here I will be only suggestive through brief attention to one episode and its surrounding circumstances. The suggestive place I want to examine may at first seem a bit unlikely—Lemuel Gulliver's pockets as he empties them for his interrogation in Lilliput. Here is an inventory of what turns up concealed on Gulliver's person:

a handkerchief
a snuffbox
a diary

a comb
a razor
a set of eating utensils
a watch
a set of pistols
a pouch of gunpowder and another pouch of bullets
silver and copper money and several pieces of gold
a pair of spectacles
a pocket perspective
and "several other little Conveniences."

*things maketh the man*

To appreciate the full effect of this pocketful, we have to re-member that Gulliver is supposed to have swum ashore—in dangerous stormy waves—with his pockets jammed like that, and he is also wearing a full set of clothes, a hat, and a large sword.

Because this information is not all presented at once, one might read the *Travels* several times, and not notice Gulliver's rich and varied cargo. Gulliver, being Gulliver, does not tell us that his swimming was impeded by his load, nor does he tell us why he hung onto the material things that connect him to his past when, buffeted by waves that threaten to scuttle him, it would have seemed sensible to discharge himself of some of his burdens. The things are, to be sure, useful to Swift in ini-tiating Gulliver's dialogue with the Lilliputians, but they are not necessary, as subsequent voyages show. Swift pretty clearly is having some fun at Gulliver's expense in making him such a dull-witted freighter, and his point seems cru-cially connected, on the one hand, to a contemporary joke, and, on the other, to Swift's perceptions about first-person narrative and the mind-numbing absurdities it sometimes of-fered to readers of contemporary narrative.

## DANIEL DEFOE'S MISTAKE

The joke was seven years old in 1726. It had involved a slip of [English author Daniel] Defoe's pen in *Robinson Crusoe*—a slip that, when corrected, still exposed a lapse in memory or lack of factual knowledge. When Defoe has Crusoe swim to the shipwreck at one point, he allows him to strip off his clothes to make the journey easier, but a little later we see Crusoe on shipboard stuffing his pockets with biscuits. Defoe later explains that Crusoe had left on his seaman's britches, but as a contemporary, Charles Gildon, pointed out, Defoe didn't thus improve his marks as a purveyor of information about seamen, for seaman's britches usually do not have pockets and even when they do, the pockets are tiny ones, much too small for biscuits: Defoe's explanation had only pinpointed and elaborated his ignorance. For Gildon, Defoe here makes Crusoe perform unlikely, even absurd actions, and his attack is on the false realism in Defoe, just as in *Gulliver's Travels* the thrust is to demonstrate what the realism and pseudo-factuality of contemporary travel accounts and fictional narratives come to at last. Gildon's joke on Defoe was, by the way, well enough known and remembered in 1725—six years after Crusoe and a year before Gulliver—that the *London Journal* can speak of the pocket episode as "a most notorious *Blunder*," which had given "Abundances of Pleasure [to] many of his Readers."

## SWIFT'S PARODY OF FIRST-PERSON NARRATIVES

Gulliver's pockets, then, work something like this: they remind us of Defoe's mistake and how authors who try to pass off genuine memoirs often are tripped by simple facts. The pockets also remind us of larger points quite beyond the comical allusion that first-person narrators, in their haste to make a point and glorify themselves, are hopelessly inaccurate, obtuse, and pretentious; that long lists and particular details do not necessarily add up to some larger truth, and that attempts to read the world and its purpose through the recording of sense impressions and the imparting of symbolic qualities to things and events . . . is finally an arrogant, self-serving, even solipsistic [regarding one's self as the only reality] way of regarding the world. *Robinson Crusoe* comes up for examination in *Gulliver's Travels* quite often in various ways: in the opening paragraph in which the particulars of Defoe's life (his career as a hosier, his imprisonment as a debtor, his prudent marriage to a woman with a large dowry) are alluded to; in the preparatory events that preface each voyage proper; in the vague motivation for Gulliver's decisions to go repeatedly to sea because of "rambling Thoughts" and an unaccountable sense of destiny; in the habitual phrases that fall from Gulliver's lips and link him repeatedly but not constantly to the consciousness of Crusoe; in the ending in which Swift provides a sharp contrast to Crusoe's homecoming. Defoe, exploring what man can do to achieve salvation and deliverance within a providential pattern, has Crusoe readjust to the com-

*(handwritten margin note:)* its more than that its about the conscious construct of the self in a narr

pany of human beings and society generally with relative ease, giving no hint that lack of conversation, human companionship, sexual relationship, and exile from the familiar for more than a quarter century offer any obtrusive problems in readjustment, and Crusoe returns to find himself remembered, beloved, and provided for by partners and well-wishers who have preserved and improved his property and investments so that he is now a rich plantation owner, soon to be a happy new husband and father. Alexander Selkirk, often said to be the prototype of Crusoe and in any case an island castaway who lived in isolation only a fraction of Crusoe's tenure, found postvoyage life far otherwise, returning to his home a silent misanthrope who avoided all company, living altogether by himself, some say in a cave he himself dug as an emblem of his psychological space. Swift's portrait of Gulliver neighing quietly to himself in his stable, unable to stand the company of his wife and children, his nose stopped with lavender, tobacco, and rue so that he cannot smell human smells, stands in sharp relief to Crusoe's homecoming and tacitly reminds us realistically of historical figures like Selkirk and of civilization and its discontents.

The example of the allusive pockets suggests that *Gulliver's Travels* is, among many other impressive things, an accreting generic or class parody not only of travel narratives per se but also of a larger developing class of first-person fictional narratives that make extraordinary claims for the importance of the contemporary, the knowableness through personal experience of large cosmic patterns, the significance of the individual, and the imperialistic possibilities of the human mind—a class parody, in short, of what we now see as the novel and the assumptions that enable it.

# Lagado: Swift's Satire of Scientific Knowledge

Clive T. Probyn

In Part III of *Gulliver's Travels* Gulliver visits the city of Lagado, home of the Projectors, a group of scientists committed to pursuing the most outlandish experiments. The Projectors satirize the Royal Society, an English scientific academy founded in 1660, whose members included the astronomer Edmund Halley (of Halley's comet fame) and Sir Isaac Newton. Though the real Royal Society engaged in many worthwhile projects, Swift's satire reveals that he believes issues of human morality should take precedence over scientific schemes, and this orientation results in his savage attack on contemporary science. Clive T. Probyn has taught at Monash University. In addition to several books on Jonathan Swift, he has written *English Fiction of the Eighteenth Century 1700–1789* and *English Poetry.*

In chapters 4 to 6 [of Part Three] Gulliver is in the metropolis of Lagado, a city of desolation and decay, but with one notable and precarious exception. Lord Munodi's estate, 'built according to the best Rules of ancient Architecture', is a symbol of perfection threatened by the modish obsession for mathematical regularity propagated by the Academy of Projectors. There are perhaps elements of [Swift's mentor, Sir William] Temple and [English political figure Henry St. John, Viscount] Bolingbroke in Munodi, each of whom disdained the world's craziness for an ideal of retirement. Tactically, Swift is exposing Gulliver to an image of traditional aristocratic culture before submerging him in the lunacies of 'Modern' mechanistic science. Of the fourteen projects in chapter 5, several are recognizable derivations from actual experiments published in the *Transactions of the Royal Society* [The Royal Society is an English academy promoting the sciences]. Many of these were included in a three-volume collection produced by Edmund Halley and William Derham in 1705–7, entitled *Miscellanea Curiosa*. Gulliver points out that the Academy of Lagado had been established 'about Forty Years ago' (i.e. in 1667, if Gulliver is recounting his experiences in 1707/8). The Royal Society received its first charter in 1662. In the first number of the *Transactions* (6 March 1665) there were the following articles:

> An Accompt of the improvement of Optick Glasses at Rome. Of the Observation made in England of a Spot in one of the Belts of the Planet Jupiter. Of the Motion of the late Comet predicted. The heads of many new Observations and Experiments, in order to an Experimental History of Cold, together with some thermometrical discourses and experiments. A relation of a very odd monstrous Calf . . . A Narrative concerning the success of the pendulum watches at sea for the longitudes; and the grant of a Patent thereupon . . .

## SWIFT'S MOCKERY OF SCIENTIFIC PROGRESS

Swift chose to isolate the oddities and ignore the possibility of a revolution in human knowledge. If some of the experiments seemed daft, others were to affect the course of human history in the profoundest possible ways. The astronomer [John] Flamsteed was a member of the Royal Society, as was [English astronomer Edmund] Halley (in 1678), and [English scientist] Sir Isaac Newton. The Society had published such seminal works as [English physicist and inventor] Robert Hooke's *Micrographia or Some Physiological Descriptions of Minute Bodies Made by Magnifying Glasses* (1665), and Newton's paper on movement (1686), out of which grew his *Principia* (1687), and also Bishop Sprat's *History of the Royal Society of London* (1667), a third of which is devoted to justifying theoretical and applied scientific research. One of its linguistic enunciations anticipated the Lagadian scheme for reducing language to things, 'by cutting Polysyllables into one, and leaving out Verbs and Participles; because in Reality all things imaginable are but Nouns'. Sprat writes that the Royal Society operates 'a constant Resolution, to reject all the amplifications, digressions, and swellings of style: to return back to the primitive purity, and shortness, when men deliver'd so many *things*, almost in an equal number of *words* . . . bringing all things as near the Mathematical plainness, as they can: and preferring the language of Artizans, Countrymen, and Merchants, before that, of Wits, or Scholars'. With a delicious social irony, the Lagadian scheme is sabotaged precisely by those groups to whom Sprat had looked for a denotative ideal, 'the Women . . . the Vulgar and Illiterate . . . Such constant irreconcileable Enemies to Science are the common People'.

Sprat, one of three bishops in the Royal Society (not to mention five doctors of divinity in a total of ninety-five Fellows), argued for the 'innocence' of experimental science and its compatibility with orthodox religious belief. Although Swift does not overtly attack the projectors on religious grounds, he nevertheless rejects the argument of 'innocence' and additionally parodies their efforts in language heavy with moral disapprobation [disapproval]. Miracles of improbability are to be achieved with very little effort; elegant mechanical theories will solve, at a stroke, complex intellectual problems; the tedium of learning and close study will be replaced by quick and easy methods available to all, irrespective of intelligence.

## THE PROJECTORS ARE OBSESSED WITH THE PHYSICAL WORLD

Swift's catalogue of scientific inanities is only apparently miscellaneous. All are connected by a perverse attempt to combine natural opposites and to discover transformations of the mundane [ordinary] or irksome into the useful and luxurious. To this extent, Swift's sub-theme is the ancient delusion that base metals can be turned into gold: his imagination plays with the extremities of intellectual aspiration out of touch with physical realities, the signs of which are bodily unpleasantness. The projectors themselves are not only deranged in the sense that their minds have abandoned their bodies, they are also dirty, smelly and unintelligible. Cucumbers may be turned into sunbeams, excrement may be recycled into its original constituents, ice may be turned into gunpowder, a blind man may be taught how to identify colours, hogs may be used to plough the fields by systematically burying their food, cobwebs may be made into silk, marble may be softened to make pincushions, and a machine has been constructed for writing books on philosophy, poetry, politics, law, mathematics and theology—all without the least intellectual qualification. Almost every scheme attempts to deny the natural and unavoidable barriers to human effort and the inevitabilities of natural processes. As an emblem of them all, the project to abandon words altogether and to substitute *things* for *words* suggests that Swift's deepest objection to experimental science is its obsession with the *physical* world at the expense of *moral* philosophy. Some members of the Royal Academy had written papers on the analogies between the two most abstract arts, music and mathematics (the Royal Academy of Music had been established in 1719), and Swift highlights this extreme form of abstract speculation as an evasion of man's primarily moral duties.

Gulliver's account of the scientists in Lagado is detached and impartial, not only because 'I had my self been a Sort of Projector in my younger Days', but also because additional satirical underlining of such gross absurdities would be strategically superfluous. But in chapter 6 Gulliver does not hesitate to evaluate the School of political Projectors as 'wholly out of their Senses'. Their attempts to match political preferment with a programme of moral virtue are dismissed as 'wild impossible Chimaeras'. Of the least lunatic, Gulliver selects those who would see an entirely physical cause for the proliferation of abstract political theories. Lagadian surgeons operate on the body politic, arguing that social faction is a disease of the individual brain:

> When Parties in a State are violent, he offered a wonderful Contrivance to reconcile them. The Method is this. You take an Hundred Leaders of each Party; you dispose them into Couples of such whose Heads are nearest of a Size; then let two nice Operators saw off the *Occiput* of each Couple at the same Time, in such a Manner that the Brain may be equally divided. Let the *Occiputs* thus cut off be interchanged, applying each to the Head of his opposite Party-Man. It seems indeed to be a Work that requireth some Exactness; but the Professor assured us, that if it were dextrously performed, the Cure would be infallible. For he argued thus; that the two half Brains being left to debate the Matter between themselves within the Space of one Scull, would soon come to a good Understanding, and produce that Moderation as well as Regularity of Thinking, so much to be wished for in the Heads of those, who imagine they came into the World only to watch and govern its Motion: And as to the Difference of Brains in Quantity or Quality, among those who are Directors in Faction; the Doctor assured us from his own Knowledge, that it was a perfect Trifle.

This ludicrously mechanical solution to an intellectual problem both ridicules those who suffer from its symptoms and deepens the dismay of those who have watched its social effects. The passage ends with a fine and dismissive irony which of course dehumanizes political leaders and at the same time suggests that in their professional life they are externalizing their own schizophrenia. In his discussion with the Laputian political theorists Gulliver's discoveries overlap with Swift's experience: the cryptographers [those who study codes] described in the last three paragraphs of chapter 6 reflect in quite precise terms the ciphers used in evidence to convict Bishop Atterbury in 1723. As if to underline the uncomfortable parallel, Gulliver's attention turns to home.

## THE IMPORTANCE OF MORAL SELF-KNOWLEDGE

Swift clearly regarded man's prime duty as moral self-knowledge. In any contest between moral philosophy and natural philosophy (or 'science'), the former takes precedence. As [English poet Alexander] Pope was to put it, 'The proper Study of Mankind is Man', and as [English writer Dr. Samuel] Johnson stated in his *Life of Milton*, 'we are perpetually moralists, but we are geometricians only by chance . . . Physical knowledge is of such rare emergence, that one man may know another half his life without being able to estimate his skill in hydrostaticks or astronomy; but his moral and prudential character immediately appears.'

For Swift the great unresolved questions about man's nature far exceeded the possible benefits from speculative and experimental science.

# CHAPTER 3

# Gulliver's Four Voyages

# Size as Metaphor in Lilliput

Jack G. Gilbert

In the first part of *Gulliver's Travels*, Gulliver is depicted
as something of a hero, a well-intentioned, naive young
man who is indoctrinated into the ways of the world. In
Lilliput, Gulliver is as magnanimous and good-natured
as he is large. He accepts the Lilliputians and shows
deference to their customs and their ruling class, even
while he might easily destroy their civilization with his
superior size and power. But the Lilliputians reveal
themselves to be as mean spirited and petty as they are
small. Instead of rewarding Gulliver as a noble public
servant, they attempt to punish him for alleged griev-
ances against the state. Throughout this first voyage,
Swift uses size as a metaphor for morality, drawing
comedy and serious meanings from the disparity in
size between Gulliver and the Lilliputians. Jack G.
Gilbert has taught at Louisiana State University. He is
the author of *Jonathan Swift: Romantic and Cynic
Moralist.*

On his first voyage Gulliver's nature proves to be as good, in
comparison with that of the Lilliputians, as his body is large.
Gulliver's merits reveal themselves from the time of his first
encounter with the little men, who appear at first in a fairly
advantageous light: they bind the sleeping Gulliver, who
awakens unable to move; and when he struggles to get loose
they subdue him with volleys of tiny arrows. He makes signs
that he is hungry and receives a generous breakfast, generous considering the size of the Lilliputians:

> I confess I was often tempted, while they were passing back-
> wards and forwards on my Body [as they carried food to his
> mouth], to seize Forty or Fifty of the first that came in my
> Reach, and dash them against the Ground. But the Remem-
> brance of what I had felt [from their arrows], which probably

Excerpted from *Jonathan Swift: Romantic and Cynic Moralist* by Jack G. Gilbert.
Copyright © 1966 by Jack G. Gilbert. Reprinted with the permission of the University
of Texas Press.

might not be the worst they could do; and the Promise of Honour I made them, for so I interpreted my submissive Behaviour, soon drove out those Imaginations. Besides, I now considered my self as bound by the Laws of Hospitality to a People who had treated me with so much Expence and Magnificence. (I, i, 5)

## GULLIVER'S MORAL STATURE

From the first, Gulliver is grateful for the kindness that he receives, even from creatures far inferior, at least in strength. Much later, even after the Emperor of Lilliput and his council decide to punish Gulliver for his well-intentioned and beneficent actions, Gulliver refuses to stoop to any base designs:

> Once I was strongly bent upon Resistance: For while I had Liberty, the whole Strength of that Empire could hardly subdue me, and I might easily with Stones pelt the Metropolis to Pieces: But I soon rejected that Project with Horror, by remembering the Oath I had made to the Emperor [swearing peace with him], the Favours I received from him, and the high Title of Nardac he conferred upon me. Neither had I so soon learned the Gratitude of Courtiers, to persuade myself that his Majesty's present Severities acquitted me of all past Obligations. (I, vii, 22)

Not only as gratitude, which Swift thought a virtue, but also as mercy and generosity, does Gulliver's benevolence come to light: chained to his quarters (an abandoned, defiled church), Gulliver becomes a center of attention, and must be guarded:

> . . . to prevent the Impertinence, and probably the Malice of the Rabble, who were very impatient to croud about me as near they durst; and some of them had the Impudence to shoot their Arrows at me as I sate on the Ground by the Door of my House; whereof one very narrowly missed my left Eye. But the Colonel ordered six of the Ringleaders to be seized, and thought no Punishment so proper as to deliver them bound into my Hands, which some of his Soldiers accordingly did, pushing them forwards with the But-ends of their Pikes into my Reach: I took them all in my right Hand, put five of them into my Coat-pocket; as to the sixth, I made a Countenance as if I would eat him alive. The poor Man squalled terribly, and the Colonel and his officers were in much Pain, especially when they saw me take out my Penknife: But I soon put them out of Fear; for, looking mildly, and immediately cutting the Strings he was bound with, I set him gently on the Ground, and away he ran. I treated the rest in the same Manner, taking them one by one out of my Pocket; and I observed, both the Soldiers and People were

highly obliged at this Mark of my Clemency, which was represented very much to my Advantage at Court. (I, ii, 3)

So favorable was the impression that the Emperor issued a commission "obliging all the Villages nine hundred Yards round the City" to furnish the victuals necessary for Gulliver's sustenance (I, ii, 1). Gradually his "Gentleness and good Behaviour" win him the trust of the natives, who "came by Degrees to be less apprehensive of any Danger from me. . . . And at last the Boys and Girls would venture to come and play at Hide and Seek in my Hair" (I, iii, 1).

Gulliver's behavior in Lilliput, even his bloodless victory over the Blefuscun fleet, is all docility, gentleness, and modesty: he returns with the enemy fleet in tow, shouting to the tiny prince, "Long live the most puissant Emperor of Lilliput!":

> His Majesty desired I would take some other Opportunity of bringing all the rest of his Enemy's Ships into his Ports. And so unmeasurable is the Ambition of Princes, that he seemed to think of nothing less than reducing the whole Empire of Blefuscu into a Province, and governing it by a Viceroy; of destroying the Big-Endian Exiles, and compelling that People to break the smaller End of their Eggs; by which he would remain sole Monarch of the whole World. But I endeavoured to divert him from this Design, by many Arguments drawn from the Topicks of Policy as well as Justice: And I plainly protested that I would never be an Instrument of bringing a free and brave People into Slavery. (I, v, 4)

The Emperor's ambition is thrown into relief by the innocence, the generosity, the magnanimity of Gulliver's attitude: like the most idealistic of the Roman republicans, or the Humanists, Gulliver will not use his power in a bad cause. The ambassadors sent from Blefuscu to sue for peace have the good sense to pay Gulliver "many Compliments" on his "Valour and Generosity" (I, v, 6) in opposing the Lilliputian Emperor's ambitions.

## GREAT TALENT EMPLOYED FOR PUBLIC GOOD

At times in Book I, Gulliver represents Swift's idea of magnanimity (appropriately in a correspondingly large body): great talents employed for public good, of such integrity as to be above any base action, and humane, generous, innocent, and modest. He seems a well-intentioned young hero, say a Telemachus [son of the Greek Hero Odysseus], who goodheartedly and awkwardly discovers the meanness of the men who make up his world. His adventures in Lilliput form the initiation of a rather idealistic young man who tries to get along in a world which he is later shocked to understand. That he has a different character in the second voyage is evident enough if we compare Gulliver's cold-blooded attempt to give the Brobdingnag king the secret of gunpowder with Gulliver's friendly warning to the Emperor of Lilliput:

I delivered up both my Pistols . . . and then my Pouch of Powder and Bullets; begging him that the former might be kept from Fire; for it would kindle with the smallest Spark, and blow up his Imperial Palace into the Air. (I, ii, 10)

His innocence is almost naïveté; it seems to me the naïveté of a young idealist: he is impressed by the bravery and the technical skill of the Lilliputians (I, i, 7; ii, 6). To the sophisticated reader Gulliver must seem an *ingénu* [an innocent]. Yet a rare *ingénu* he is! Of gigantic comparative strength, he ingenuously wonders at physical distinctions among the little men: the Emperor, he observes "is taller by almost the Breadth of my Nail, than any of his Court; which alone is enough to strike an Awe in the Beholders" (I, ii, 3). Gulliver's modesty is almost so excessive as to be craven: the Lilliputians chain him like a dog, and Gulliver becomes a friendly animal, an affable freak, who entertains the populace or the court with his appetite or his handkerchief. Gulliver prostrates himself before the emperors of Blefuscu and Lilliput, yet dares to tell the latter that he will not help "force the Consciences, or destroy the Liberties and Lives of an innocent People" (I, vii, 9).

With his humanistic attitude toward war, Gulliver is willing to fight to defend the Emperor and his country against invaders; but he will not pursue the war simply for the glory to be got at the cost of enslaving a free people. The parallel to the Tory attitude toward [English general considered among history's greatest military leaders] Marlborough's continental campaigns against France is clear; the Tories were the "Lovers of Peace," Swift believed.

### THE PUBLIC SERVANT'S FATE

Since Gulliver is given a good character in Lilliput, it is said that he represents not just Swift's ethical preferences, but some actual persons he admired—either [Swift's friends] [Robert] Harley [First Earl of Oxford], or [Henry] St. John, or both. . . .

If Gulliver resembles in important facets the magnanimous men whom Swift admired, one action of his becomes a hieroglyph of the fate of the too highly gifted public servant. Swift criticized, while he admired, the great men of affairs who sought to achieve some public good by means of an uncommon or daring policy (even as they labored under the burden of a general envy of their superiority). The "Infelicity" of such magnanimous statesmen (as Themistocles, Aristides, Scipio, Sir Walter Raleigh, Bacon, Clarendon, Strafford, Laud, Oxford, and Bolingbroke), their fall from power or their disgrace, Swift believed "to have been caused by their Neglect of common Forms, together with the Contempt of little Helps, and little Hindrances; which is made by [English philosopher Thomas] Hobbes the Definition of Magnanimity; And the Contempt, as it certainly displeases the People in generall, so it giveth Offence to all with whom such Ministers have to deal".

Consider then Gulliver, like one of Swift's magnanimous men, in a moment of great exigency: the palace of Lilliput has caught fire. With little helps, buckets "about the Size of a large Thimble," which are almost little hindrances because they do "little Good," Gulliver tries to put out the fire:

> The Case seemed wholly desperate and deplorable; and this magnificent Palace would have infallibly been burnt down to the Ground, if, by a Presence of Mind, unusual to me, I had not suddenly thought, of an Expedient. I had the Evening before drank plentifully of a most delicious Wine . . . which is very diuretick. By the luckiest Chance in the World, I had not discharged myself of any Part of it. . . . Which I voided in such a Quantity, and applied so well to the proper Places, that in three Minutes the Fire was wholly extinguished; and the rest of that noble Pile, which had cost so many Ages in erecting, preserved from Destruction. (I, v, 9)

Gulliver's adventures are an allegory of the fate of the magnanimous, modest, good-natured, and benevolent public servant, whose good actions (perhaps a little out of common forms) result in punishment by the petty, ungrateful, unjust, and vicious men whom he helps.

### THE PETTY VICIOUSNESS OF THE LILLIPUTIANS

Gulliver rendered two great services to the Emperor of Lilliput: he destroyed the enemy fleet which threatened Lilliput, and he extinguished the fire and preserved at least parts of the palace. But in both instances Gulliver was to suffer by the ingratitude and injustice of courts. In the first, Gulliver's republicanism and love of liberty prevented his acquiescing in the Emperor's military ambitions:

> And from this Time began an Intrigue between his Majesty, and a junta of Ministers maliciously bent against me, which . . . had like to ha\ve ended in my utter Destruction. Of so little Weight are the greatest Services to Princes, when put into the Balance with a Refusal to gratify their Passions. (I, v, 5)

In the instance of the fire, just as in the preliminary arrangements for the Peace of Utrecht [series of treaties that concluded the war of Spanish succession], a great good was achieved in not so honorable or usual a manner:

> And I was privately assured, that the Empress conceiving the greatest Abhorrence of what I had done, removed to the most distant Side of the Court, firmly resolved that those Buildings should never be repaired for her Use; and, in the Presence of her chief Confidents, could not forbear vowing Revenge. (I, v, 10)

Gulliver's reward, then, for two benefactions is death for treason, as outlined in the articles of impeachment drawn up by the Emperor and his ministers in secret (I, vii, 6 ff.). Gulliver's "friend," Reldresal, has argued with the ministers for mercy, and suggests that the criminal be only blinded; finally, it is resolved that the official published punishment is to be blinding, while the secret intention is to starve him after he is blinded: "Thus by the great Friendship of the Secretary [Reldresal], the whole Affair was compromised" (I, vii, 18). Their injustice is as great as their ingratitude; but justice is a thing unknown in that court, where preferences go not to virtue, but "Dexterity" or nimbleness: offices and honors are "earned" by cutting capers on tight ropes or in leaping over and creeping under a baton held by the Emperor (I, iii, 2–4). . . .

The Lilliputians are remarkable for their cruelty: Skyresh Bolgolam takes great pleasure in forcing "Articles and Conditions" upon Gulliver before he is set free (I, iii, 8); the Emperor is anxious to conquer Blefuscu and thereby "to destroy and put to death not only all the Big-Endian Exiles [his own people], but likewise all the People of that Empire, who would not immediately forsake the Big-Endian Heresy" (I, vii, 9); the Emperor's advisors are resourceful and zestful in imagining ways to murder their benefactor, Gulliver; Reldresal stands by his friend and asks that he *only* be blinded. Similar viciousness they direct against each other, for in politics there are "Animosities" over the great issue of the height of one's heels; and in religion the bitterest controversy has raged over which end of the egg is to be cracked first, according to their bible. The issues between the High-Heels and Low-Heels, and the Big-Endians and Little-Endians have generated bloody persecutions and the protracted war between Lilliput and Blefuscu (I, iv). By means of such symbols as the breaking of eggs and the height of heels, Swift not only makes the satirical point that religious and political questions are usually per se inconsequential, but also reveals the quarrels over trifles actually result from contentious, litigious viciousness.

As ludicrous as the disparity between such trifling issues and the wars they become is the diminutive stature of the Lilliputians, when compared to their pride or vanity; the Emperor of this little people is known as the

> Delight and Terror of the Universe, whose Dominions extend five Thousand Blustrugs, (above twelve Miles in Circumference) to the Extremities of the Globe: Monarch of all Monarchs: Taller than the Sons of Men; whose Feet press down to the Center, and whose Head strikes against the Sun. (I, iii, 9)

Gulliver's presence accentuates the folly of such pretensions.

# Size and Social Values in Brobdingnag

Howard Erskine-Hill

As readers embark upon the second voyage with Gulliver, they like the main character. Readers identify with him and tend to admire the manner in which he has conducted himself in Lilliput. Now readers worry about Gulliver. If he has suffered in the hands of the Lilliputians, how badly will he be tortured by the giant Brobdingnagians? But Gulliver is treated remarkably well by the giants, and it is he who is reduced to ethical inferiority, particularly when he lauds the culture of Europe, which the Brobdingnagian king finds horrific. Because readers have identified with Gulliver, the king's repudiation of him and his society becomes a rejection of the reader as well. Readers are abruptly forced to lose sympathy for the main character even as they must question their own morality. Howard Erskine-Hill has taught at the University of Cambridge, England. He is the author of numerous books on British literature including several on Swift and Alexander Pope.

The reader embarks upon the Voyage to Brobdingnag with certain expectations. First, we expect a clear, practical, physical narrative which will familiarize, if not demystify, the marvelous. Secondly, we are now well-disposed to Gulliver. On the basis of Part I we expect in him a character well-disposed and civil towards any strange peoples he may encounter, but not merely a passive follower of their ways. We think Gulliver has a mind of his own, and a capacity for moral independence and individual action.

These expectations are, and are not, fulfilled. Having adjusted to the diction of Part I the reader is jolted somewhat to encounter, early in Part II, a passage of sheer tarpaulin [common sailor talk]:

Finding it was like to overblow, we took in our Sprit-sail, and stood by to hand the Fore-sail; but making foul Weather, we looked the Guns were all fast, and handed the Missen. The Ship lay very broad off, so we thought it better spooning before the Sea than trying or hulling. We reeft the Foresail and set him, we hawled aft the Fore-sheet; the Helm was hard a Weather. The Ship wore bravely. We belay'd the Foredown-hall; but the Sail was split, and we hawl'd down the Yard, and got the Sail into the Ship, and unbound all the things clear of it. It was a very fierce Storm; the Sea broke strange and dangerous. We hawl'd off upon the Lanniard of the Wipstaff . . . .

and so on for as much again. Dampier [English pirate and writer] acknowledged that he had 'divested' himself of 'Sea-Phrases' to gratify the 'Land Reader; for which the Seamen will hardly forgive me' (preface to *A New Voyage*). Swift, perhaps, takes this opportunity of displaying Gulliver's professional familiarity with 'Sea-Phrases', but the sudden plunge into nautical language (for which Swift had plundered a passage in Samuel Sturmy's *Mariner's Magazine* 1669) is irresistibly comic and, like the Utopian discourse in 'A Voyage to Lilliput', is a sign of Swift's unashamed readiness to change his mode when the right opportunity occurs. His narrative has thus a variable relation with the world.

## INTO THE WORLD OF THE BROBDINGNAGIANS

Almost at once Gulliver reverts to his usual narrative clarity and plain style for a transition into the marvellous. What follows is a triumph of the commonplace and almost casual manner. Having landed on a barren and rocky coast to look for water and finding none, Gulliver returns to the shore only to see 'our Men already got into the Boat, and rowing for Life to the Ship. I was going to hollow after them, although it had been to little purpose, when I observ'd a huge Creature walking after them in the Sea, as fast as he could . . .' Running inland in terror, he sees from high ground a meadow with grass twenty feet tall. He comes to a field of corn 'rising at least forty Foot' and 'Trees so lofty that I could make no Computation of their Altitude'. The monsters who now come to reap the harvest are as tall as church spires and with voices like thunder high in the air. In a desperate attempt to hide from them and escape, Gulliver squeezes himself between the corn stalks until he comes to a part where the corn has been laid by rain and wind. Here he cannot get through, the fallen ears pierce his clothes and hurt him, and as the giant reapers draw near he lies down wholly 'overcome by Grief and Despair.' As he waits to be discovered, like a small wild creature from the last corner of the harvest field, he is able to reflect on how he had appeared to the Lilliputians as these monsters now appeared to him. It is a most interesting moment, establishing Gulliver's mental continuity between the two different worlds of the first two Parts. An educated man, he recalls those philosophers (most recently Swift's countryman [Irish philosopher George] Berkeley) who have taught that 'nothing is great or little otherwise than by Comparison', but neither this, nor his own recollections of Lilliput can eradicate from his mind the totally inconsistent opinion that the larger creatures are the 'more Savage and cruel in Proportion to their Bulk . . .' Nothing can be more natural than that Gulliver, in his present crisis, should expect 'to be a Morsel in the Mouth of the first among these enormous Barbarians who should happen to seize' him, yet *he* had not behaved barbarously to Lilliput or Blefuscu, while Lilliput had planned to behave barbarously to him. Gulliver is unable to put his two experiences together so as to come to an adequate comparative judgement. Meanwhile one of the giant reapers looks as if he will tread on Gulliver by accident, Gulliver screams, and the reaper spots him, pausing to consider 'with the Caution of one who endeavours to lay hold on a small dangerous Animal in such a Manner that it shall not be able either to scratch or bite him; as I my self have sometimes done with a *Weasel* in *England*.' Swift has managed Gulliver's transition into a new world of wonders with extraordinary physical and psychological imagination.

Whatever he expects, Gulliver is not devoured by the giant reaper. He is treated gently enough. But he becomes the possession of the local farmer, and is shown for money around the country inns as a midget monster. Eventually he is taken to the capital, Lorbulgrud, where he comes to the attention of the royal court. His health breaking down 'by the continual Drudgery of entertaining the Rabble every Hour of the Day', Gulliver manages to attract the sympathy of the Queen. In response to her question whether he would like to come and live at Court, Gulliver, in a moment comparable to that between [Robinson and his Servant] Crusoe and Friday, says he is his master's 'Slave' but, if free, would be proud to devote his life to her 'Service'. The Queen then purchases him, and Glumdalclitch, the farmer's nine-year-old daughter, who was the first Brobdingnagian to be kind to him and look after him, is allowed to stay with him at Court.

## COMPARISON TO LILLIPUT

'A Voyage to Brobdingnag' is not only different from 'A Voyage to Lilliput' in its reversal of the physical relation of Gulliver with his host people, though that is its simplest and most striking effect. In Part I Gulliver uses a giant's strength with care, judgement and success. In the grip of a military crisis, Lilliput affords him the opportunity to act and a dramatic relation develops between the two, in which Gulliver becomes first the hero, then the alleged traitor, of Lilliput. Brobdingnag, by contrast, is a stable country. There is no external enemy, while internal dissensions between monarch, nobles and people have been happily compromised by the grandfather of the present King. In Brobdingnag Gulliver's capacity as a man of action is limited either to mere performance for the interest of spectators, or self-defence in ridiculous and humiliating situations. The reader, whose sympathies with Gulliver have been endorsed by the outcome of the previous Part, shares a measure of his frustration at a predicament in which energy and action can achieve nothing. Part II proceeds in two main ways. First it focuses on the inevitable humiliations of Gulliver and on his midget's eye view of the physical life of the giants. Secondly but more importantly it concentrates on something that never happened in Lilliput: the long series of conversations between Gulliver and the King concerning society and government. Here we come to see that if the physical action of Part II is little more than a series of frustrations, it constitutes a psychological action of considerable interest. It will be right to give brief consideration to each of these aspects of the book.

## PHYSICAL ISSUES

Gulliver's first show of bravery (it may be thought) was when he outfaced the farmer's wife's fierce-looking, purring, cat (three times larger than an ox): the cat drew back. Soon after, he is assailed at night by two rats and kills one with his sword, wounding the other. This is comparable to slaying certain dragons. On another occasion 'a small white' Brobdingnagian 'Spaniel' (a well-trained dog) follows his scent, picks him up in its mouth, and brings him faithfully to its master. Much less pleasant is the pet monkey belonging to one of the Clerks of the Kitchen which carries Gulliver off, though Glumdalclitch eventually rescues him. A stream of such incidents, including much trouble with small birds and flies, stretches through most of Part II. Swift gives them great emphasis. Some of these episodes are recounted with special humour. Gulliver himself, who shows occasional signs of reverting to the mentality of a small boy, ruefully recounts how, finding a 'Cowdung' in his path, 'I must needs try my Activity by attempting to leap over it.' Of course he jumps short and returns home 'filthily bemired.' This is another moral episode in miniature, like Flimnap's capering on the tightrope, but the humour lies in the embarrassed tone of Gulliver's subsequent narrative ('I must needs try my Activity . . .'). After Gulliver sails his boat in the artificial pond made for him, to the delight of the Queen and her ladies, Glumdalclitch always carries the boat into her closet and hangs it 'on a Nail to dry.' The Court dwarf ('I verily think he was not full Thirty Foot high') is a particular trial to Gulliver, always affecting to swagger and look big when he passes him, and seldom failing 'of a smart Word or two upon my Littleness; against which I could only revenge myself by calling him *Brother*, challenging him to wrestle; and such Repartees as are usual in the Mouths of *Court Pages*.' This humour is perhaps the very foundation of *Gulliver's Travels* though it is generally more understated, often developed satirically, and sometimes tragically.

More disconcerting than Gulliver's many humiliations, which the kindly Glumdalclitch retails to the laughing royal family and court, is Gulliver's vision of the bodily life of the giants. This is not just a matter of size but of what the microscopic eye can see. In another significant recollection of Lilliput, Gulliver recalls a friend of his there finding a close view of his face 'a very shocking Sight': 'great Holes' apparent in his skin, bristles stronger than those of a boar, and unpleasant differences of colour. This is now how Gulliver sees the Brobdingnagians. The Lilliputians had seemed to Gulliver 'the fairest in the World' but now a horror of fleshly life is revealed to him: 'the Woman with a Cancer in her Breast, swelled to a monstrous Size, full of Holes . . . a Fellow with a Wen in his Neck, larger than five Woolpacks . . . But, the most hateful Sight of all was the Lice crawling on their Cloaths: I could see distinctly the Limbs of these Vermin. . . .' Unfortunately the horror is not confined to the diseased and poor. The Queen is a moderate and fastidious eater, but the sight of her at dinner is to Gulliver terrifying. The maids of honour are young, healthy and beautiful. Since they hardly see in Gulliver a serious sexual partner, they do not hesitate to strip and dress in his presence: their skin appears coarse, with 'Hairs hanging from it thicker than Pack-threads.' Swift here becomes outrageously surreal in combining the sexually titillating with the disconcerting: Gulliver does not appreciate being set, by the best-looking and most 'frolicksome' maid of honour, 'astride upon one of her Nipples. . . .' The reader is likely to be divided in response to this moment. The wider implications, in which Swift is seen to be a Rabelais [French satirist] with a remarkably different feeling about the physical, show him writing as an heir of the French philosopher [René] Descartes and the English poet [English satiric poet John Wilmot, Earl of] Rochester, both well known to Swift. In each case the sheer rigour of their sceptical analysis led them to the *impasse* which a twentieth-century philosopher, Gilbert Ryle, has memorably designated the error of 'the Ghost in the Machine': the spirit in the body. They could not see, as some earlier thinkers and poets could, the spiritual *expressed* by bodily life, bodily life lending vigour to the life of the spirit. Gulliver's un-Rabelaisian, microscopic eye in Brobdingnag, his fastidious and world-weary eye in the land of the Houyhnhnms, is the eye that has envisioned one of the most terrifying things the world can display to human view: living but unanimated matter, the 'Wen . . . larger than five Woolpacks', mindless growth.

## CONVERSING WITH THE KING

This mind-and-body dilemma is underlined when we turn to the second aspect of Part II, the conversations between Gulliver and the King of Brobdingnag. Unlike the Emperor of Lilliput the King is interested to hear what Gulliver can tell him about Europe. Gulliver himself introduces the first conversation in a thoroughly candid way, paying tribute to the King's clear apprehension, exact judgements and wise observations, while at the same time admitting that he himself had been 'a little too copious in talking of my own beloved Country', its trade, wars, schisms, parties and prejudices. Gulliver here plays something of the part of Reldresal in Lilliput, though unlike the Lilliputian he does not have an urgent political motive for his discourse. By the same token Gulliver's serious practical response to Reldresal is contrasted with that of the giant king to Gulliver:

> he could nor forbear taking me up in his right Hand, and stroaking me gently with the other; after an hearty Fit of laugh-

ing, asked me whether I were a *Whig* or a *Tory*. Then turning
to his first Minister, who waited behind him with a white Staff,
near as tall as the Mainmast of the Royal *Sovereign*, he observed, how contemptible a Thing was human Grandeur,
which could be mimicked by such diminutive Insects as I . . .
And thus he continued on, while my Colour came and went
several Times, with Indignation to hear our noble Country, the
Mistress of Arts and Arms, the Scourge of France, the Arbitress
of Europe, the Seat of Virtue, Piety, Honour and Truth, the Pride
and Envy of the World, so contemptuously treated.

This passage is wonderfully structured around the idea of relative scale, and the corresponding political implications. Gulliver, in the palm of the King's hand, suddenly discloses (in his
subsequent narrative) the physical height of the Minister's symbol of authority ('as tall as the Main-mast of the Royal *Sovereign*'): the issue of [opposing English political parties] Whig or
Tory (to which Swift had committed much of his life) is then
made the object of hearty laughter and Gulliver is called a
diminutive insect. The reader's vision has been made to focus
down, enlarge and focus down again, before Gulliver, turning
red and pale by turns with mortification, vainly attempts to enlarge the minds of his hearers with the alleged greatness of his
native land. It will be noticed that what the King finds contemptible is something in his own world: human grandeur. His
line of thought is to find something in the discourse of a
stranger that he can apply to his own situation, though it is not
of course what Gulliver hopes he will learn. Somehow Gulliver
cannot avoid getting laughed at. Worse is to come. Wearied with
entertaining the Court and being an object of ridicule, he remarks to the King one day 'That, Reason did not extend itself
with the Bulk of the Body', that among other animals bees and
ants had the reputation of being more wise and industrious
than many larger creatures, and that even he, Gulliver, might
give the King information which would be valuable to him. . . .
True to this humanist ideal, the giant King listens attentively
while Gulliver wishing for the Tongue of [Greek orator]
Demosthenes or [Roman statesman and orator] Cicero,
launches into 'the Praise of my own dear native Country'.

## GULLIVER'S DESCRIPTION OF ENGLAND

We have already seen Gulliver in the rather misleading rôle of
Utopian narrator, in chapter 6 of Part I. Swift now rings a further change on this idea. Gulliver does not consider his discourses properly Utopian; from his viewpoint he is offering a

well-deserved panegyrical [elaborately praising] history of Great Britain. From the King's point of view, on the other hand, inclined as he is to think that Britain may exist, listening to Gulliver is like Morus listening to Hythloday in [Sir Thomas More's] *Utopia.* Gulliver covers every aspect of the political and social structure of this allegedly ideal commonwealth; it takes five interviews to get through it all, and the King makes a lot of notes. Then, in a sixth interview, the King asks questions and makes his own observations. These remarks are admirably telling and practical, and are a form of satire in themselves. On the topic of new promotions to the nobility the King asked: 'Whether the Humour of the Prince, a Sum of Money to a Court-Lady, or a Prime Minister; or a Design of strengthening a Party opposite to the Publick Interest, ever happened to be Motives in those Advancements'? The humour and irony lie in the words 'ever happened'. Again, the King asked about how and why people in Britain sought to become members of the House of Commons [lower house of English Parliament]: 'How it came to pass, that People were so violently bent upon getting into this Assembly, which I allowed to be a great Trouble and Expense, often to the Ruin of their Families, without any Salary or Pension: Because this appeared such an exalted Strain of Virtue and publick Spirit, that his Majesty seemed to doubt it might possibly not be always sincere'. Here the humour lies not only in the tentativeness of the concluding question (set against the obviousness of the evidence), but in our uncertainty as to whether the King or Gulliver is responsible for the delicacy of formulation. On the legal system of Britain the King, in a more decisive question, asked: 'Whether Party in Religion or Politicks were observed to be of any Weight in the Scale of Justice.' As to the recent history of Gulliver's native land, 'he was amazed to hear me talk of a mercenary standing Army in the midst of Peace, and among a free People' and, of 'our Affairs during the last Century' protested that the history was only 'an Heap of Conspiracies, rebellions, Murders, Massacres, Revolutions, Banishments . . .'. In a seventh and final interview the King sums up his conclusions. He is willing to accept that Gulliver himself, a traveller, may have escaped many of the vices of his country but, he says, in the most quoted passage from the whole of the *Travels,* 'I cannot but conclude the Bulk of your Natives, to be the most pernicious Race of little odious Vermin that Nature ever suffered to crawl upon the Surface of the Earth.'

At this Gulliver is filled with resentment. He admits to art-fully eluding the thrust of the King's questions so far as possi-ble, and to presenting his native land in the most favourable possible light. We perceive that the King's devastating criti-cisms are a blend of obvious generalization on self-interest in public life and of specific Tory positions on matter such as standing armies and war, taxes and the national debt. Gul-liver, by contrast, now emerges as a devious patriot and a ranting Whig [pro-war party], resolved to dismiss the King's substantial objections to the condition of Britain as the *'Nar-rowness* of *Thinking'* inevitable in a King 'wholly secluded from the rest of the World . . .'. Gulliver's idea is now not to ar-gue back, certainly not to admit he is in the wrong, but to 'in-gratiate' himself further in the King's favour by offering him something powerful. He seeks to compel the King's respect by giving him the secret of gunpowder, describing with some rel-ish the effect of this invention, and how useful it might be to the monarch if his metropolis should ever 'pretend to dispute his absolute Commands'. The King is 'struck with Horror at the Description I had given of these terrible Engines . . . A strange Effect of *narrow* Principles and *short Views!'*

## THE READER IS GUILTY, TOO

Swift's larger strategy in Parts I and II now comes clearly into view. He has been working all the time with the reader's view-point in mind. In Part I Gulliver (save a little solemn naivety) won the approval of the reader by his conduct and judgement. His goodwill, and moderation, and the real danger he is in at the end, win as much sympathy from the reader as the hero of such an impossible tale could possibly gain. At the begin-ning of Part II, therefore, the reader is inclined to identify with Gulliver and, despite implications to the contrary, to share his evident fear that if the diminutive Lilliputians ended by treat-ing him badly, the monstrous Brobdingnagians are bound to treat him worse. This barbarous treatment does not come about. Once at court he is kindly treated though an object of repeated ridicule. The reader continues to identify with Gul-liver, laughing at him indeed, but uncomfortably aware of how we should feel in his shoes, until the time of Gulliver's political conversation with the King. Then our sympathy with him is in a few pages completely shattered: indeed, the King's condemnation is felt the more strongly because the reader has been so close to Gulliver. Swift's shaping of the fable of

Parts I and II has deprived the reader of any position of detachment from which the King's judgement could be assessed. The satirical rhetoric of Swift's first two voyages has turned entirely on this issue of identification with and alienation from Gulliver. We realize that we are 'the most pernicious Race of little odious Vermin that Nature ever suffered to crawl upon the Surface of the Earth' and that it is Gulliver's implausible and excessive patriotism, glorification of war and admiration of power, that has brought this judgement down on us.

## THE PHYSICAL AND THE MORAL

The symmetries of Swift's first two voyages are not therefore merely physical: Gulliver the giant among midgets, Gulliver the midget among giants. We see that the physical situation affects the moral outlook. It is easier for Gulliver to be moderate and benevolent in Lilliput, despite the vicious ingenuity of the Lilliputians, than to be so in Brobdingnag, where his very size means that he is perpetually laughed at and humiliated. Thus the steady Tory of Part I becomes the war-crazed Whig of Part II. It is also notable that the Emperor of Lilliput only wants to use Gulliver as the ultimate weapon in his war. The King of Brobdingnag, on the other hand, pays attention to all that Gulliver tells him. He really hopes to learn something, especially on fiscal policy. The Emperor of Lilliput is the Tory view of a Whig king. The King of Brobdingnag is the Tory view of a Tory king, that is to say he governs a stable and peaceful commonwealth, without party, and his judgements only take on a contentious edge when controverting some Whig innovation of which Gulliver informs him. The King is the father of his people, but his kingdom is still (though gigantic) part of the real world: there is disease, poverty, greed and vanity. Finally the two books contrast with and complement each other in regard to the relation between Gulliver and the reader, the trust which has grown up through Part I being broken by the end of Part II.

Still, Gulliver longs to regain what it is natural for him to think of as his 'Liberty' and to return to his family ('those domestick Pledges') in his native land. This wish is accomplished, not through any effort on Gulliver's part, but in a wonderful and Cyrano-like way. One day at the seaside a giant eagle carries away Gulliver's traveling box with Gulliver inside. In due course it is dropped into the sea, from which he is fortunate enough to be rescued by an English ship which brings him home. The captain will take no payment for his passage and even lends Gulliver five shillings. Gulliver has no religious thoughts on what many would have considered a providential deliverance, but comments darkly on the 'evil Destiny' which would take him again to sea. Meanwhile he feels like a giant and everyone else seems to him like a pigmy.

# Lilliput and Brobdingnag: Swift's Experiments in Optics

W.A. Speck

Gulliver's trips to Lilliput and Brobdingnag allow
Swift to compare and contrast three cultures: the two
fictional worlds and the real Europe. Swift is able to
draw humor as well as serious philosophy by dimin-
ishing and magnifying human beings. The larger humans appear, the more physically flawed they seem
to be, for example. Yet even though Lilliput and
Brobdingnag are not utopias, European culture and
Europeans themselves continually fare badly when
compared with these imaginary worlds. W.A. Speck
has taught at the University of Newcastle upon Tyne.
He is the author of numerous books on eighteenth-
century history and literature, including *The Birth of
Britain: A New Nation, 1700–1710* and *London Politics, 1713–1717*.

Dr. Johnson's remark to Boswell, 'When once you have
thought of big men and little men it is very easy to do all the
rest', is in a way the most inadequate comment ever passed on
*Gulliver's Travels*. In another way, however, it does hit the
main point of the first two voyages squarely and firmly on the
head. Swift carefully contrived the contrasts and comparisons
between Gulliver, the Lilliputians and the Brobdingnagians.
In Lilliput Gulliver found that an English inch was equivalent
to a Lilliputian foot. In Brobdingnag the ratio was exactly reversed, an English foot corresponding to a Brobdingnagian
inch. Thus the average Lilliputian man was 'somewhat under
six inches', while a Brobdingnagian giant was some seventy
feet tall. As in Brobdingnag so in Lilliput Nature observed 'the
same Proportion through all her Operations'. This enabled

Swift to make observations about human behaviour which were both comic and philosophical.

## SWIFT'S COMEDY

The comic possibilities are mainly exploited in the voyage to Lilliput, which presumably explains why it is the most popular, especially with children. They can identify themselves with the Lilliputians, and enjoy the ways in which the little men get the better of Gulliver. Such incidents as his first meal, in which he consumed basketfuls of meat and two hogsheads of wine, and the taking of the inventory of his possessions, when one of the inspectors stepped up to his knees in snuff, have a wider appeal. One of the funniest incidents, however, is expurgated [censored] in children's editions–the march of the Lilliputian army through the triumphal arch of Gulliver's legs.

Though comic episodes are not so frequent in the second voyage they occur often enough to make one realise why Swift's contemporaries regarded *Gulliver's Travels* as a merry book. They were surely amused by the passage wherein Gulliver is taken home by the Brobdingnagian farmer, who shows him to his wife, 'but she screamed and ran back as women in England do at the sight of a Toad or a Spider'. When she recovers from the shock she lets Gulliver sit at their table, and while they eat off plates 'twenty-four feet across,' he eats scraps, all the time afraid that he will fall off the thirty foot high table, 'which gave them exceeding Delight'.

The account of the meal also delights the reader, until towards the end Gulliver describes his horror at seeing a nurse feeding a baby:

> I must confess no Object ever disgusted me so much as the Sight of her monstrous Breast . . . This made me reflect upon the fair Skins of our *English* Ladies, who appear so beautiful to us, only because they are of our own Size, and their Defects not to be seen but through a magnifying Glass, where we find by Experiment that the smoothest and whitest Skins look rough and coarse, and ill coloured.

## AN EXPERIMENT IN OPTICS

The first two voyages offer just such an experiment in optics. The big men and the little men might have been suggested to Swift by [Irish philosopher George] Bishop Berkeley's *Theory of Vision*. Berkeley had pointed out that the idea of size was not fixed but relative to the observer. Gulliver reflected in Brobdingnag:

> Undoubtedly Philosophers are in the right when they tell us,
> that nothing is great or little otherwise than by Comparison: It
> might have pleased Fortune to let the *Lilliputians* find some
> Nation, where the People were as diminutive with respect to
> them, as they were to me. And who knows but that even this
> prodigious Race of Mortals might be overmatched in some dis-
> tant Part of the World, whereof we have yet no Discovery?

One of the effects of magnification and diminution is to
make big men look hideous and small men look handsome.
This comes out most strikingly in Gulliver's revolting description of the beggars which he saw in the capital of Brobdingnag. Of course his remarks were not merely relevant to
the giants. It has been suggested that Gulliver's revulsion reflects Swift's own reaction to the sight of the beggars in
Dublin. Gulliver was himself aware that his observations
would be equally valid if applied to his own people.

> I REMEMBER when I was at *Lilliput*, the Complexions of those
> diminutive People appeared to me the fairest in the World: And
> talking upon this Subject with a Person of Learning there, who
> was an intimate Friend of mine; he said, that my Face appeared
> much fairer and smoother when he looked on me from the
> Ground, than it did upon a nearer View when I took him up in
> my Hand, and brought him close; which he confessed was at
> first a very shocking Sight. He said, he could discover great
> Holes in my Skin; that the Stumps of my Beard were ten Times
> stronger than the Bristles of a Boar; and my Complexion made
> up of several Colours altogether disagreeable.

> Part II, Chapter I

Physically the Lilliputians might appear to be near perfect
specimens in contrast with the Brobdingnagians, but morally
the big men compared favourably with the little men, even
though Gulliver expected them to be worse:

> For, as human Creatures are observed to be more Savage and
> cruel in Proportion to their Bulk; what could I expect but to be
> a Morsel in the Mouth of the first among these enormous Bar-
> barians who should happen to seize me?

## COMPARISONS AND CONTRASTS OF THREE CULTURES

The purpose of Swift's moral satire in the first two voyages is
complicated by the fact that he used the inhabitants of Lilliput
and Brobdingnag both to contrast and to compare with Europeans. When contrasted with the little and the big people Europeans come off badly. In comparison all three are shown in
an unfavourable light.

There are more comparisons than contrasts in Lilliput. Indeed, apart from the obvious difference in size there are few differences between the Lilliputians and the English. Only in Chapter six do they appear as Utopian beings, who enjoyed ideal legal, administrative and educational systems. Their laws were enforced not only by punishment but also by rewards:

> Whoever can there bring sufficient Proof that he hath strictly observed the Laws of his Country for seventy-three Moons, hath a Claim to certain Privileges, according to his Quality and Condition of Life, with a proportionable Sum of Money out of a Fund appropriated for that Use: He likewise acquires the Title of *Snilpall*, or *Legal*, which is added to his Name, but doth not descend to his Posterity. And these People thought it a prodigious Defect of Policy among us, when I told them that our Laws were enforced only by Penalties, without any Mention of Reward . . .
>
> Part I, Chapter 6

As for the administration: 'In chusing Persons for all Employments, they have more regard to good Morals than to great Abilities . . .' Finally, on education:

> . . . their Opinion is, that Parents are the last of all others to be trusted with the Education of their own Children: And therefore they have in every Town publick Nurseries, where all Parents, except Cottagers and Labourers, are obliged to send their Infants of both Sexes to be reared and educated . . . These Schools are of several kinds, suited to different Qualities, and to both Sexes.

These ideals accord with the views on legislation, government and education which Swift himself had urged in pamphlet and letter for years.

The Utopian passages in Chapter six of the first part are out of tune with the rest of the narrative. Swift himself as good as admitted that they did not harmonise when he got Gulliver to write:

> In relating these . . . Laws, I would only be understood to mean the original Institutions, and not the most scandalous Corruptions into which these People are fallen by the degenerate Nature of Man.

Throughout the rest of the book most Lilliputians display characteristics which would have justified Gulliver had he passed the same judgment on them as the King of Brobdingnag did upon the English:

> I cannot but conclude the Bulk of your Natives, to be the most pernicious Race of little odious Vermin that Nature ever suffered to crawl upon the surface of the Earth.

The king's judgment was delivered after a series of conversations during the course of which Gulliver described the government of Great Britain to him. Gulliver gave the king an idealised account of British institutions, but the king asked a number of questions which probed beyond the ideal to the reality. Thus Gulliver described how the House of Commons consisted of 'principal Gentlemen, freely picked and culled out by the People themselves, for their great Abilities, and Love of their Country, to represent the Wisdom of the whole Nation . . .', which the king countered with the queries:

> Whether, a Stranger with a strong Purse might not influence the vulgar Voters to chuse him before their own Landlord, or the most considerable Gentleman in the Neighbourhood. How it came to pass, that People were so violently bent upon getting into this Assembly, which I allowed to be a great Trouble and Expence, often to the Ruin of their Families, without any Salary or Pension: Because this appeared such an exalted Strain of Virtue and publick Spirit, that his Majesty seemed to doubt it might possibly not be always sincere: And he desired to know, whether such zealous Gentlemen could have any Views of refunding themselves for the Charges and Trouble they were at, by sacrificing the publick Good to the Designs of a weak and vicious Prince, in Conjunction with a corrupted Ministry.

Part II, Chapter 6

Such queries were a fair enough comment on the practice of the unreformed parliamentary system. In this fashion government and above all justice are exposed as being as corrupt as Parliament.

## DEDUCING SWIFT'S VIEWS

Swift's own views on these institutions are not very easy to deduce. Even Gulliver's exact opinions are not crystal clear, for he admits that he 'would hide the Frailties and Deformities of my Political Mother, and place her Virtues and Beauties in the most advantageous Light'. However, we can be reasonably certain that even Gulliver's real views are several degrees too naïve to represent Swift's. At the same time we cannot with confidence say that Swift's opinions are the same as the king's. Those who argue that Swift always chose a *via media* [middle way] between extremes would say that while Gulliver makes British institutions too pure the king makes them too corrupt by half. On the other hand it is singular that the king's attitude is essentially that of the independent Tory gentleman whom Swift so much admired; viz. his opposition to the upkeep of a standing army in peacetime, and his distrust of lawyers and monied men. It seems most probable, therefore, that Swift did share the king's attitudes, not to say prejudices. There is no parallel for this passage in the first voyage, and indeed Europe is contrasted much more with Brobdingnag than with Lilliput. Gulliver gives an account of Brobdingnagian laws and military affairs, which are every bit as Utopian as those of Lilliput, though he himself is somewhat scornful of them. When he offers to show them how to make cannon:

> THE King was struck with Horror at the Description I had given of those terrible Engines, and the Proposal I had made. He was amazed how so impotent and grovelling an Insect as I (these were his Expressions) could entertain such inhuman Ideas, and in so familiar a Manner as to appear wholly unmoved at all the Scenes of Blood and Desolation, which I had painted as the common Effects of those destructive Machines; whereof he said, some evil Genius, Enemy to Mankind, must have been the first Contriver. As for himself, he protested, that although few Things delighted him so much as new Discoveries in Art or in Nature; yet he would rather lose Half his Kingdom than be privy to such a Secret; which he commanded me, as I valued my Life, never to mention any more.

> (A Strange Effect of *narrow Principles* and *short Views* . . .)
>
> Part II, Chapter 7

Though the king's horror at the effects of cannon imply that he, and presumably Swift, had pacifist leanings, there was nevertheless an army in Brobdingnag, or rather a militia of 176,000 foot and 32,000 horse. Gulliver was himself:

> curious to know how this Prince, to whose Dominions there is no Access from any other Country, came to think of Armies, or to teach his People the Practice of military Discipline. But I was soon informed, both by Conversation, and Reading their Histories. For, in the Course of many Ages they have been troubled with the same Disease, to which the whole Race of Mankind is Subject; the Nobility often contending for Power, the People for Liberty, and the King for absolute Dominion. All which, however happily tempered by the Laws of that Kingdom, have been sometimes violated by each of the three Parties; and have more than once occasioned Civil Wars, the last whereof was happily put an End to by this Prince's Grandfather in a general Composition; and the Militia then settled with common Consent hath been ever since kept in the strictest Duty.

> Part II, Chapter 7

Such passages compare rather than contrast Brobdingnag with England. Though they are relatively fewer in the second voyage nevertheless there are passages in which the big men act no more virtuously than the Lilliputians. The exploitation of Gulliver by the farmer, though understandable, is not particularly commendable. The same can be said of his treatment at the hands of the Maids of Honour. One of the most spectacular sights which Gulliver saw in Brobdingnag was the execution of a murderer.

By alternately comparing and contrasting Europe with Lilliput and Brobdingnag Swift made the most of his experiment with optics. The comparisons between Lilliput and Europe make human pretensions seem petty and contemptible. Those between Europe and Brobdingnag make human beings appear gross and disgusting. On the other hand English institutions and customs seem corrupt and degenerate in contrast with those of the big men and the little men.

# Hopeless Worlds: The Third Voyage

Michael DePorte

Michael DePorte provides an overview of the third part of *Gulliver's Travels*, examining the countries of Laputa, Lagado, Glubbdubdrib, and Luggnagg and explaining the significance of each. DePorte reminds the reader that this part of *Gulliver's Travels* was actually written last, after Swift had completed the Houyhnhnms section. In each of the countries in Part III reason has run out of control. DePorte suggests that Swift may have written this section to contrast its foolishness with the pure reason of the Houyhnhnms so that readers would not believe that he was satirizing Houyhnhnms' society. Nevertheless, while magical horses may live a life of pure reason, perfection is not a human attribute. Gulliver's attempts to mimic Houyhnhnms' lifestyle are as ludicrous as the Projectors' scientific experiments in book three. Michael DePorte has taught at the University of New Hampshire. He is the author of *Nightmares and Hobbyhorses: Swift, Sterne, and Augustan Ideas of Madness.*

Book 3 may lack the immediate power of the other books, but it has a delayed power derived in some measure from its narrative defects: because the connections between parts are not always clear we must work them out, and we cannot work them out unless we consider fully what they mean.

## LAPUTA: WORLD WITHOUT HOPE

The name of Gulliver's third unlucky ship, the *Hopewell*, provides a significant clue to the concerns that underlie this voyage. Whether we take it as a sardonic injunction (hope well!) or as a reference to psychic terrain (the well of hope),

Excerpted from "Teaching the Third Voyage," by Michael DePorte, in *Approaches to Teaching Swift's "Gulliver's Travels,"* edited by Edward J. Rielly. Copyright © 1988 by The Modern Language Association of America. Reprinted with the permission of The Modern Language Association of America.

the name suggests that book 3 is about hope, or rather, about hope running dry. For each of the lands Gulliver visits turns out to be a land of false promise. Book 3 is Swift's satire on wishful thinking.

Let us examine hope first in its utopian aspect. Laputa and Lagado explode the sentimental view of science and technology as tickets to future utopias. The flying island is a material success. Control of flight has given the islanders security from invasion and domination of the mainland below. They live, Gulliver says, surrounded by "Plenty and Magnificence" on the "the most delicious Spot of Ground in the World." But their privileged position brings them no joy; worship of science has poisoned every aspect of Laputan life. The astronomers exhaust themselves in speculation, the chief fruit of which is a terror of cosmic disaster that keeps them awake nights. In their obsession with the future they have lost the most precious of the future's gifts: hope. They drag along in a stupor of anxiety, unable to take pleasure in friends and family, let alone in the bounty around them. Marriage in Laputa is an unrelieved catastrophe. The astronomers are such miserable companions that their wives run off at the earliest opportunity; any other life is preferable. Recently, the wife of the prime minister forsook the luxuries of her position to dwell in squalor on the mainland with an old, deformed footman who beat her daily.

## FALSE HOPE IN LAGADO

The calamities of the Laputans are largely psychological; those of their disciples at Lagado largely physical. The projectors are hopeful enough, but the countryside is in ruins, the people starving, and they themselves no closer to their goals than when they began. The grand old projector of the academy, "*the universal Artist*," who for thirty years has devoted himself to "the Improvement of human Life," has such passion for his projects that he never considers how naked sheep or solidified air will benefit humankind should he succeed in producing them. The only projects that do not seem crackbrained are those that steer clear of technology and seek to advance society by intelligent application of what is known already about human nature: treat statesmen for physical and mental diseases that may affect their conduct of office; tax individuals on their vices or, better yet, on the qualities (generally vices as well) they esteem in them-

**MEANINGS OF THE NAME "LAPUTA"**

*Swift was fond of puns and word games, and the name "Laputa" takes on a number of meanings in this light.*

The name *Laputa* itself may suggest a dystopia or, rather, a perversion of utopia. Speculation on the process by which Swift invented names is perhaps a dubious enterprise but, since he enjoyed puns, anagrams, and near-anagrams, his reader is entitled to consider those he finds, if not to look for them. *Laputa* is a near-anagram of *utopia*. *Utopia* means *nowhere*. *Nowhere* contains an anagram of *whore*. *Laputa* means *whore*.

Jenny Mezciems, "The Unity of Swift's 'Voyage to Laputa': Structure as Meaning in Utopian Fiction" in Claude Rawson, ed. *Jonathan Swift: A Collection of Critical Essays*. Englewood Cliffs, NJ: Prentice Hall, 1995, p. 247.

selves; choose public officials for their wisdom and virtue. Note the trap Swift lays here for napping readers by embedding sane ideas amid crazy ones and by having Gulliver call the proposal for virtuous government the looniest he ever heard of. As always, inconsistency is crucial to Swift's satire. We cannot assume that because every project at Lagado thus far has been nutty all of them will be, nor that because Gulliver's responses in Laputa and Lagado have thus far been sensible they will continue to make sense. The promise of high science and applied technology is heady: to cut loose from the past and soar into new regions of possibility. What Lagado and Laputa in fact offer is a choice between fake hope and foolish despair.

## GLUBBDUBDRIB AND THE MYTH OF PAST PERFECTION

Gulliver's encounter with the dead in Glubbdubdrib addresses the antithetical but equally sentimental desire to embrace the past as mother of all excellence. On casual reading, the revelations of the departed appear to support just this view of history. When asked to assess the rival theories of [French philosopher] Gassendi and [French philosopher] Descartes, [Greek philosopher] Aristotle magisterially dismisses them both. When Gulliver summons the senate of Rome to present itself alongside a modern legislature, the one impresses him as an "assembly of Heroes and Demy-Gods," the other as a "Knot of Pedlars, Pick-pockets, Highwaymen and Bullies." Looking back on the revelations of the dead, Gulliver reports that he "was chiefly disgusted with modern History." But if the Ancients generally come across better than the Moderns we must not forget that Sir Thomas More is listed in the "*Sextumvirate*" of incomparable worthies and that a good deal of what Gulliver picks up from the dead is uncongenial to idealized visions of antiquity. Alexander the Great confides that he died a drunkard, Caesar that Brutus did the world a favor by stabbing him. The one unrewarded patriot whose story Gulliver chooses to tell lived in Rome's golden age and was slighted by Augustus [the Emperor] himself. For Swift, utopia is no more a province of long ago than a province of the future. He may share with lovers of the past the view that progress is a desperate, tawdry illusion, but he wants no part of their consolation. To muse on the perfections of a golden age while accepting decay as inevitable is to school oneself to compliance: what one cannot fight, one need not fight.

### THE STRULDBRUGGS' FEARFUL ETERNITY

The satire on pipe dreams reaches its culmination with the account of the Struldbruggs. Here Swift confronts humanity's deepest longing—to elude death—and he prepares the ground with care. When Gulliver learns that there are people in Luggnagg who live forever he cannot contain himself; he bursts into raptures at the thought of men living free of the "Weight and Depression of Spirits caused by the continual Apprehension of Death" and eagerly outlines what he would do with immortality: First, he would amass wealth. With careful investments he should have no trouble becoming the richest man in the kingdom after a few hundred years. Next, he would acquire learning. By pursuing a diligent program of reading and keeping a detailed political and cultural record of passing times he would eventually know more than anyone else in the kingdom, at which point he and like-minded Struldbruggs might form a council to advise humankind. It is the chance to benefit society that fires Gulliver's imagination. The instruction and example of these godlike beings would, Gulliver says, "probably prevent that continual Degeneracy of human Nature, so justly complained of in all Ages." On top of all this, he could have the satisfaction of seeing "great Inventions brought to the utmost Perfection"—the discovery of perpetual motion, for instance, or of the "*universal Medicine.*"

As a Struldbrugg, Gulliver believes, he would have everything to hope for. In reality, of course, he would have nothing to hope for. So far are Struldbruggs from escaping the "Depression of Spirits" attendant upon ordinary life that at thirty they sink into a depression from which they never emerge. For it is then Struldbruggs begin to contemplate what fate has in store: loss of health, loss of friends, loss of status, loss of reason and memory, an eternity of Alzheimer's disease. After seeing a few Struldbruggs Gulliver is "heartily ashamed of the pleasing Visions" he formed of immortality and swears that "no Tyrant could invent a Death into which [he] would not run with Pleasure from such a Life." The Struldbruggs are, significantly, the last exotic people Gulliver meets before his voyage to Houyhnhnmland. They afford a peculiarly horrifying demonstration of the point Swift makes throughout book 3: dreams of perfectibility, whether vested in utopias of the future or golden ages of the past, are just that—dreams. The human condition is hostile to perfection. The Struldbruggs prepare us for what is to come: anything perfect must, by implication, be other than human.

This brings us to consider the place book 3 occupies in the plan of the *Travels*, an issue best approached by reminding students that book 3 was written last. More often than not this fact has been used to explain the apparent miscellaneousness of the voyage, the apparent dispersion of energy. Swift, the argument runs, had various secondary targets he had not gotten around to attacking. Having reached the climax of his satire in book 4, he could relax and lark about on lesser hobbyhorses [topics with which one is obsessed].

## Contrasting True Reason and False

But there is another, more interesting explanation. Swift may have written book 3 because he felt something important was missing. Perhaps he feared book 4 might be taken to burlesque the life of reason and added his new book to furnish unmistakable examples of reason run amok. And though "soft" readings of the fourth book [which claim Swift was satirizing the Houyhnhnms' society] hardly support such speculation, we should remember that until the last fifty years no one viewed the Houyhnhnms as possible targets of satire and that arguments to prove them targets typically require a good deal of finesse. Without book 3 it would surely be easier to maintain that wholly rational societies like that of the Houyhnhnms are meant to seem ludicrous and unpleasant.

As it stands, the contrast with the Laputans shows the difference between true reason and false. Dissension among Houyhnhnms is unknown because among them reason is true reason, and true reason will always lead those who employ it to the same conclusions. The Laputans, however, are "vehemently given to Opposition"; they dispute "every Inch of Party Opinion" and are keenest when, as is commonly the case, they know nothing whatever of the matter. Indeed, it is the Laputans, not the Houyhnhnms, who are narrowly rational. In poetry, Gulliver says, Houyhnhnms "must be allowed to excel all other Mortals"; Laputans are such complete strangers to "Imagination, Fancy, and Invention" that they do not even have words for them in their language. As we have seen, high science betrays the Laputans into a nightmare of tedium and neurotic dread. It also opens a back door to superstition: on the sly, they cast horoscopes. Unlike Houyhnhnms, who value friendship and society, Laputans reject the claims of feeling altogether. They aspire to a purely mental existence, and their passions, denied legitimate outlets, exact an appropriate revenge.

The abuse of reason, obvious in the preoccupations of the Laputans and experiments of the projectors, is also a recurring motif in Gulliver's meeting with the shades: misguided commentators on [Greek poet] Homer and Aristotle, kings who contend "with great Strength of Reason" that corruption is essential to government, philosophers who reduce the mysteries of nature to logical systems.

The recurrent lesson of book 3, that a life of pure reason lies beyond human endeavor, is central to the meaning of the *Travels.* It is also preeminent among the many lessons Gulliver fails to learn. He becomes at the end a martyr to wishful thinking. The letter to his cousin Sympson leaves no doubt that the Gulliver who as a youth had "been a Sort of Projector," has embarked on a project worthy of Lagado. There is nothing wrong with getting spiders to spin colored silk, bottling sunbeams against cloudy days, or confecting delicacies from excrement, except that such enterprises fail. Nor is anything wrong in trying to make Houyhnhnms of men save the hopelessness of it, which drives one mad.

# The Limitations of the Houyhnhnms

Boris Ford

In considering the fourth part of *Gulliver's Travels*, Boris Ford rejects the so-called "hard reading" of the novel, which suggests that the Houyhnhnms are idealized rational creatures who Swift believes humanity should emulate. Instead, Ford points out the satire and wit of Part IV, and suggests the weaknesses inherent in Houyhnhnm society. In doing so, his opinion represents the "soft reading" of the novel, which sees the Houyhnhnms as a satirical artistic device that mocks mankind. Boris Ford has taught at Cambridge University and Sheffield University in England.

There is no work by Swift over which such revealing and significant differences of opinion occur as the last book of *Gulliver's Travels*. To the kind of reader who inclines towards the 'Augustan' [18th century] view of him, this book is a straight attack on the filthy degradation of the human species in the name of 'Nature and Reason'; and, in so far as Gulliver (who is Swift) rejects humanity, it is the work of a misanthropist. 'Jonathan Swift aimed at mankind the most venomous arrow that scorn has ever yet let loose', writes Mr Carl van Doren, whose very readable biography is marred by the excessive prominence given to the misanthropic and tormented side of his nature. But if we see Swift first and foremost as a wit, skilled in the elaboration of ideas which do not directly represent his own beliefs, we may arrive not only at a more satisfactory interpretation of this book, but also at a more acceptable view of its author.

## THE SITUATION IN BOOK FOUR

In this book a piquant situation is presented to us, which may be stated as follows: 'In the real world the gift of reason is bestowed upon human beings and withheld from animals. In the land of

Excerpted from *The Pelican Guide to English Literature*, vol. 4, *From Dryden to Johnson*, edited by Boris Ford (London: Penguin, 1957). Reprinted with the permission of David Higham Associates Limited.

the Houyhnhnms reason has been given to horses and withheld from—.' Here we naturally pause, but we are intended to continue: ". . . withheld from human beings.' The Yahoos are human beings, without the gift of reason. Into this world comes Gulliver, different from both in that he is a human being with reason. An important factor is that everything is seen and judged from the Houyhnhnms' angle: it is their country and their point of view imposes itself. Gulliver is alone and unique. Anxious to make his hosts understand that he is not a Yahoo, he must abide the test of the physical evidence, which is against him, and here Swift, by a peculiarly inhuman detachment in his use of detail, makes us see him as the Houyhnhnms see him:

> . . . he then stroaked my Body very gently and looked round me several Times, after which he said it was plain I must be a perfect *Yahoo*; but that I differed very much from the rest of my Species, in the softness and whiteness and smoothness of my Skin, my want of Hair in several parts of my Body, the Shape and Shortness of my Claws behind and before, and my Affectation of walking continually on my two hinder Feet.
>
> (Ch. III.)

Gulliver's superiority in the matter of reason is, however, recognized; but this leads to graver embarrassment. He is obliged to give an account of the uses to which reason is put in those lands where human beings dominate. Swift takes advantage of the fact that the Houyhnhnms know nothing of wickedness, so that everything has to be explained in detail. This device, of presenting the facts as they would have to be presented to an uninitiated listener, must be regarded as one of the modes of artistic distortion. It enables Swift to order his details in an ominous way, to secure heightening and emphasis. What purports to be a cold, purely matter-of-fact statement becomes a fearful concentration of images:

> What you have told me (said my Master) upon the Subject of War, does indeed discover most admirably the Effects of that Reason you pretend to: However, it is happy that the *Shame* is greater than the *Danger;* and that Nature hath left you utterly incapable of doing much Mischief: For your Mouths lying flat with your Faces, you can hardly bite each other to any Purpose, unless by Consent. Then as to the Claws upon your Feet before and behind, they are so short and tender, that one of our *Yahoos* would drive a Dozen of yours before him. And therefore in recounting the Numbers of those who have been killed in Battle, I cannot but think that you have *said the Thing which is not.*

> I could not forbear shaking my Head and smiling a little at his ignorance. And, being no Stranger to the Art of War, I gave

him a Description of Cannons, Culverins, Muskets, Cara-
bines, Pistols, Bullets, Powder, Swords, Bayonets, Battles,
Sieges, Retreats, Attacks, Undermines, Countermines, Bom-
bardments, Sea-fights; Ships sunk with a Thousand Men;
twenty Thousand killed on each Side; dying Groans, Limbs
flying in the Air: Smoak, Noise, Confusion, trampling to
Death under Horses' Feet; Flight, Pursuit, Victory; Fields
strewed with Carcases left for Food to Dogs and Wolves, and
Birds of Prey; Plundering, Stripping, Ravishing, Burning, and
Destroying. And to set forth the Valour of my own dear Countrymen, I assured him that I had seen them blow up a Hundred Enemies at once in a Siege, and as many in a Ship, and
beheld the dead Bodies come down in Pieces from the
Clouds, to the great Diversion of the Spectators.
(Ch. V.)

## HUMANS ARE WORSE THAN YAHOOS

Human beings are superior to Yahoos, then, mainly in their
capacity for mischief. We are obliged to consider the Yahoos
in a new light. They are more primitive than human beings,
more openly filthy; but are not human beings, with their
complicated diseases, capable of even worse physical nasti-
ness? Swift presents us with a number of descriptions of Yahoo behaviour, provokingly reminiscent of human behaviour but cruder; more contemptible in one sense, and yet
more harmless. For example, Yahoo avarice:

> . . . in some Fields of his Country, there are certain shining *Stones*
> of several Colours, whereof the *Yahoos* are violently fond; and
> when part of these Stones are fixed in the Earth, as it sometimes
> happeth, they will dig with their claws for whole Days to get them
> out, and carry them away, and hide them by Heaps in their Ken-
> nels; but still looking round with great Caution, for fear their
> Comrades should find out their Treasure. My Master said, he
> could never discover the Reason of this unnatural Appetite, or
> how these *Stones* could be of any Use to a *Yahoo*; but now he be-
> lieved it might proceed from the same Principle of *Avarice*, which
> I had ascribed to Mankind; that, he had once, by way of Experi-
> ment, privately removed a Heap of these *Stones* from the Place
> where one of his *Yahoos* had buried it: whereupon, the sordid
> Animal missing the Treasure, by his loud lamenting brought the
> whole Herd to the Place, there miserably howled, then fell to bit-
> ing and tearing the rest; began to pine away, would neither eat
> nor sleep, nor work, until he ordered a Servant privately to con-
> vey the *Stones* into the same Hole, and hide them as before;
> which when his *Yahoo* had found, he presently recovered his
> Spirits and good Humour; but took Care to remove them to a bet-
> ter hiding Place; and hath ever since been a very serviceable
> Brute.

(Ch. VII.)

There are similar pictures of the Yahoo treatment of a fallen favourite and a Yahoo female sexually excited. It is the human equivalent that we are continually confronted with in these descriptions. The Yahoo is a mirror in which human nature must see itself. Swift's technique here may be regarded as an extended example of the device of 'arguing through images'. The Yahoo is the image of man, but distorted: man with a difference. Each picture of the Yahoo reminds us of the odious resemblance, but if we try to escape from it by insisting on the difference we come up against another set of images, of human behaviour, which show us what the difference really amounts to. . . .

The conclusion which Swift has forced us to entertain—that man is virtually a Yahoo or worse—is impossible and outrageous. Clearly some trick of logic has been practised upon us, and we must try to find out what it is. Where has Swift deviated

## THE HOUYHNHNMS' LIFESTYLE HAS ITS ATTRACTIONS

*Denis Donoghue takes exception to the "soft" reading of* Gulliver's Travels, *which suggests that the Houyhnhnms are merely objects of Swift's satire. Their simple, rational lifestyle would have been attractive to Swift, who might have given up much to attain it.*

Readers of *Gulliver's Travels* are often led to conclude that the Houyhnhnms are objects of Swift's satire just as much as the Yahoos; that the cool, passionless existence they have devised is monstrous, rationalist, Deist [a theology based solely on reason]. This may or may not be true: my own reading of the book suggests that, far more than we have allowed, the life of the Houyhnhnms embodies Swift's desire for ease and rest. To be relieved of passion he was prepared to pay a high price. At one point we read:

> As these noble Houyhnhnms are endowed by Nature with a general Disposition to all Virtues, and have no Conceptions or Ideas of what is evil in a rational Creature; so their grand Maxim is, to cultivate Reason, and to be wholly governed by it. Neither is Reason among them a Point problematical as with us, where Men can argue with Plausibility on both Sides of a Question; but strikes you with immediate Conviction; as it must needs do where it is not mingled, obscured, or discoloured by Passion and Interest.

It is perverse to discount the implications here, either because they apply to the invalidated Houyhnhnms or because the from a true view of human nature to achieve this distortion? What is the relevant fact about man which he has succeeded in misrepresenting or suppressing? The answer will vary according to whether we resort to Christian orthodoxy or not. To a Christian, which Swift was, the relevant facts would be man's moral weakness owing to the Fall and the need for Christian charity in judging him. A modern, non-theological answer might be that man, in his development from primitive forms of life, has achieved only a limited rationality and morality, so that a measure of failure in all human beings must be expected.

## THE HOUYHNHNMS ARE NOT EQUIPPED TO JUDGE

Swift's strategy is to cause man to be judged by creatures who are unequipped to understand him sympathetically. The Houyhnhnms, living the placid life of reason, neither troubled nor inspired by irrational forces, know nothing of

words come from the equally suspect Gulliver. Whatever we have made of Gulliver or the Houyhnhnms up to this point, the fact remains that a situation in which reason operates by instinct would be a happy situation and one particularly congenial to Swift. It is not fanciful to assume that Swift's feelings are accurately implied at this point, regardless of Gulliver's limitation. For the moment, it seems fair to say, Gulliver's sentiments and Swift's have coincided: there is no discernible irony. This does not mean that, as an invariable rule, Swift endorses Gulliver; nor does it mean that in every respect and in every consideration he endorses the Houyhnhnms. In plural form we have to accustom ourselves to live from moment to moment. Even in the passage on instinctive reason it is better not to take the words as attaching themselves to the Houyhnhnms, in the sense that a trait of character attaches itself to the man who possesses it; but rather as a relevant sentiment, locally pointed for contrast. The fact that the sentiment is invoked at that moment is more important than that it is attached to the Houyhnhnms. The words have more to do with human limitation, by reflection and contrast, than with Houyhnhnm merit. Certainly it is possible to detach the sentiment easily enough from Gulliver: we are to apply it to ourselves rather than to him. The force which connects it to Gulliver is not of primary importance; its bearing upon us, upon the rational sense of mankind, is far more significant.

Denis Donoghue, *Jonathan Swift: A Critical Introduction*, Cambridge: Cambridge University Press, 1969, pp. 14–15.

the indignity or the glory of the human state. They are on a different metaphysical level from man: there is no equivalent to the Fall in their history. But, as we have seen, it is their sense of values which imposes itself. The great mistake, surely, is to suppose that Swift seriously intended the Houyhnhnm standard to be applied to man. The Houyhnhnms are a device for embarrassing mankind. That Gulliver, the plain man who seems to represent average human nature, should be converted to the Houyhnhnms'standpoint is simply a part of Swift's strategy. It is also part of the strategy that Gulliver, in giving an account of the human race, should omit important truths which would have explained the more disgraceful side of the picture.

## LIMITATIONS OF THE HOUYHNHNMS

What do the Houyhnhnms represent? They may perhaps remind us of the impossible and inhuman standard of perfection which people sometimes apply to their fellow-men when they are feeling unreasonable. It is part of Swift's witty purpose here to be unreasonable. Can they represent his ideal of moral perfection? To say so is to bring his sense of values seriously into question, for the Houyhnhnms are in several respects unsympathetic, even repellent. They feel no sorrow at the death of their relatives; they marry according to the wishes of parents and friends, knowing nothing of love and courtship; and they seem depressingly deficient in urges and enthusiasms such as make life exciting, if less orderly, for human beings. As Dr [F.R] Leavis wittily expresses it, 'they may have all the reason, but the Yahoos have all the life. . . . The clean skin of the Houyhnhnms, in short, is stretched over a void. He identifies them with, 'Reason, Truth and Nature, the Augustan positives', but claims that, 'it was in deadly earnest that Swift appealed to these'. This would imply that Swift's art is at fault, that he fails to make his point with us because his positives are thinner and less satisfying than he realizes. But is there not some injustice here? To a sensibility as much outraged by disorder and dirt as Swift's, mere order and cleanliness must have had an appeal, but this does not mean that they were his 'positives', any more than incidental, even frequent, exasperation at human behaviour is to be labelled 'misanthropy'. One has to distinguish here between the beliefs and attitudes to which the author, as a responsible moral being, commits himself, and those very different, sometimes livelier, reactions which are a matter of temperament, and which often lend themselves irresistibly to artistic treatment. It was easier in Swift's period than later for the author to step down from one level of attitude to the other, and it is the healthier state of affairs that this should be natural. The need to distinguish between the two levels is very important for readers of Swift, and the failure to do so is a frequent occasion for misunderstanding. The Houyhnhnms were an idea to be played with, offering scope for the indulgence of temperamental animus, but not to be taken too seriously. Is there not a slight humorous awareness in the suavity with which he dwells on their solemn simplicity and innocence?

# CHAPTER 4

# Reactions and Continuing Relevance

READINGS ON
GULLIVER'S TRAVELS

# In Defense of Jonathan Swift

William Hazlitt

William Hazlitt, an essayist of the English Romantic era of the nineteenth century, responds to the harsh criticism of Swift by writers such as Samuel Johnson. With keen insight, and, at times, ironic cleverness, Hazlitt asserts that Swift's message may not have been the most pleasant to listen to, but that it was honest and brilliantly executed. Swift did not hate mankind; he loved it the way parents love an unruly child. Pointing out the wrongs in human affairs is not equivalent to misanthropy, Hazlitt suggests. It was simply not in Swift's nature to lavish empty praise when there were so many wrongs all around him. While many critics have attacked Swift more for his character than his writings, Swift's genius was in his character; it was his harsh, angry temperament that produced the brilliant satire in his writings.

Swift's reputation as a poet has been in a manner obscured by the greater splendour, by the natural force and inventive genius of his prose writings; but if he had never written either the "Tale of a Tub" or "Gulliver's Travels," his name merely as a poet would have come down to us, and have gone down to posterity with well-earned honours. His "Imitations of Horace," and still more his Verses on his own Death, place him in the first rank of agreeable moralists in verse. There is not only a dry humour, an exquisite tone of irony, in these productions of his pen, but there is a touching, unpretending pathos, mixed up with the most whimsical and eccentric strokes of pleasantry and satire. His "Description of the Morning in London," and of a "City Shower," which were first published in the *Tatler*, are among the most delightful of the contents of that very delightful work. Swift

Excerpted from *William Hazlitt: Essayist and Critic: Selections from his Writings*, by Alexander Ireland (London and New York: Frederick Warne, 1889).

shone as one of the most sensible of the poets; he is also distinguished as one of the most nonsensical of them. No man has written so many lackadaisical, slipshod, tedious, trifling, foolish, fantastical verses as he, which are so little an imputation on the wisdom of the writer, and which, in fact, only show his readiness to oblige others and to forget himself. . . . The "Tale of a Tub" is one of the most masterly compositions in the language, whether for thought, wit, or style. It is so capital and undeniable a proof of the author's talents, that Dr. [Samuel] Johnson, who did not like Swift, would not allow that he wrote it. It is hard that the same performance should stand in the way of a man's promotion to a bishopric, as wanting gravity, and at the same time be denied to be his, as having too much wit. It is a pity the Doctor did not find out some graver author, for whom he felt a critical kindness, on whom to father this splendid but unacknowledged production. Dr. Johnson could not deny that "Gulliver's Travels" were his; he therefore disputed their merits, and said that, after the first idea of them was conceived, they were easy to execute; all the rest followed mechanically. I do not know how that may be; but the mechanism employed is something very different from any that the author of "Rasselas" [a prose satire by Johnson] was in the habit of bringing to bear on such occasions. There is nothing more futile, as well as invidious, than this mode of criticising a work of original genius. Its greatest merit is supposed to be in the invention; and you say very wisely, that it is not *in the execution.* You might as well take away the merit of the invention of the telescope by saying that, after its uses were explained and understood, any ordinary eyesight could look through it. Whether the excellence of "Gulliver's Travels" is in the conception or the execution is of little consequence; the power is somewhere, and it is a power that has moved the world. The power is not that of big words and vaunting commonplaces. Swift left these to those who wanted them, and has done what his acuteness and intensity of mind alone could enable any one to conceive or to perform. His object was to strip empty pride and grandeur of the imposing air which external circumstances throw around them; and for this purpose he has cheated the imagination of the illusions which the prejudices of sense and of the world put upon it, by reducing everything to the abstract predicament of size. He enlarges or diminishes the scale, as he wishes to show the insignificance or the grossness of our overweening self-love. That he has done this with mathematical precision, with complete presence of mind, and perfect keeping, in a manner that comes equally home to the understanding of the man and of the child, does not take away from the merit of the work or the genius of the author. He has taken a new view of human nature, such as a being of a higher sphere might take of it; he has torn the scales from off his moral vision; he has tried an experiment upon human life, and sifted its pretensions from the alloy of circumstances; he has measured it with a rule, has weighed it in a balance, and found it, for the most part, wanting and worthless—in substance and in show. Nothing solid, nothing valuable is left in his system but virtue and wisdom. What a libel is this upon mankind! What a convincing proof of misanthropy! What presumption and what *malice prepense* [malice designed or before deliberated], to show men what they are, and to teach them what they ought to be! What a mortifying stroke aimed

### Dr. Johnson's Distaste for Jonathan Swift

*Renowned eighteenth-century writer and scholar Samuel Johnson had little regard for Swift and even less for* Gulliver's Travels. *Here Johnson's biographer, James Boswell, relates a scene during which Johnson displayed his disdain for Swift.*

Johnson was in high spirits this evening at the club, and talked with great animation and success. He attacked Swift, as he used to do upon all occasions. 'The "Tale of a Tub" is so much superiour to his other writings, that one can hardly believe he was the authour of it. There is in it such a vigour of mind, such a swarm of thoughts, so much of nature, and art, and life.' I wondered to hear him say of "Gulliver's Travels," 'When once you have thought of big men and little men, it is very easy to do all the rest.' I endeavoured to make a stand for Swift, and tried to rouse those who were much more able to defend him; but in vain. Johnson at last, of his own accord, allowed very great merit to the inventory of articles found in the pockets of the Man Mountain, particularly the description of his watch, which it was conjectured was his God, as he consulted it upon all occasions. He observed, that 'Swift put his name to but two things, (after he had a name to put,) "The Plan for the Improvement of the English Language," and the last "Drapier's Letter."'

James Boswell, *Boswell's Life of Johnson*, George Birkbeck Hill and L.F. Powell, eds. Oxford: Clarendon, 1970, pp. 318–19.

at national glory is that unlucky incident of Gulliver's wading across the channel and carrying off the whole fleet of Blefuscu! After that, we have only to consider which of the contending parties was in the right. What a shock to personal vanity is given in the account of Gulliver's nurse, Glumdalclitch! Still, notwithstanding the disparagement to her personal charms, her good-nature remains the same amiable quality as before. I cannot see the harm, the misanthropy, the immoral and degrading tendency of this. The moral lesson is as fine as the intellectual exhibition is amusing. It is an attempt to tear off the mask of imposture from the world; and nothing but imposture has a right to complain of it. It is, indeed, the way with our quacks in morality to preach up the dignity of human nature, to pamper pride and hypocrisy with the idle mockeries of the virtues they pretend to, and which they have not; but it was not Swift's way to cant morality or anything else; nor did his genius prompt him to write unmeaning panegyrics [elaborate praise] on mankind! . . .

## LAUGHING AT PAIN

The ludicrous in Swift arises out of his keen sense of impropriety, his soreness and impatience of the least absurdity. He separates with a severe and caustic air truth from falsehood, folly from wisdom, "shows vice her own image, scorn her own feature;" and it is the force, the precision, and the honest abruptness with which the separation is made that excites our surprise, our admiration, and laughter. He sets a mark of reprobation on that which offends good sense and good manners which cannot be mistaken, and which holds it up to our ridicule and contempt ever after. His occasional disposition to trifling (already noticed) was a relaxation from the excessive earnestness of his mind. *Indignatio facit versus* [anger made against]. His better genius was his spleen. It was the biting acrimony of his temper that sharpened his other faculties. The truth of his perceptions produced the pointed coruscations of his wit; his playful irony was the result of inward bitterness of thought; his imagination was the product of the literal, dry, incorrigible tenaciousness of his understanding. He endeavoured to escape from the persecution of realities into the regions of fancy, and invented his Liliputians and Brobdignagians, Yahoos and Houynhyms, as a diversion to the more painful knowledge of the world around him: *they* only made him laugh, while men and women made him angry. His feverish impatience made him view the infirmities of that great baby, the world, with the same scrutinising glance and jealous irritability that a parent regards the failings of its offspring; but, as Rousseau has well observed, parents have not on this account been supposed to have more affection for other people's children than their own. In other respects, and except from the sparkling effervescence of his gall, Swift's brain was as "dry as the remainder biscuit after a voyage."

# Gulliver's Travels Is the Product of a Sick Mind

William Makepeace Thackeray

Nineteenth-century English satiric novelist William Makepeace Thackeray admired the genius in Swift's writing, but he had little use for the man behind the work. While Thackeray ably points out some of the hilarious passages in *Gulliver's Travels*, he is deeply disturbed by the overall message, particularly the misanthropy of Part IV. What type of mind could have conceived, however satirically, of eating children as a solution for human hunger in Swift's essay "A Modest Proposal"? Similarly, Thackeray wonders what depraved mind could have turned humans into Yahoos, with all the self-hatred such a transformation implies. Despite his genius as a writer, Swift should be reviled for his dark vision of mankind. William Makepeace Thackeray is regarded as one of the great English novelists. His books include *Vanity Fair, Barry Lyndon,* and *Pendennis.*

The "sæva indignatio" [referring to Swift's self-composed epitaph, "He has gone where fierce indignation can lacerate his heart no more . . ."] of which [Swift] spoke as lacerating his heart, and which he dares to inscribe on his tombstone— as if the wretch who lay under that stone waiting God's judgment had a right to be angry—breaks out from him in a thousand pages of his writing, and tears and rends him. Against men in office, he having been overthrown; against men in England, he having lost his chance of preferment there, the furious exile never fails to rage and curse. Is it fair to call the famous "Drapier's Letters" [Swift's political writings] patriotism? They are master-pieces of dreadful humour and invective: they are reasoned logically enough too, but the proposition is as monstrous and fabulous as the Lil-

Excerpted from *The Works of William Makepeace Thackeray,* vol. 26, by William Makepeace Thackeray (New York: George D. Sproule, 1904).

liputian island. It is not that the grievance is so great, but there is his enemy—the assault is wonderful for its activity and terrible rage. It is Samson, with a bone in his hand, rushing on his enemies and felling them: one admires not the cause so much as the strength, the anger, the fury of the champion. As is the case with madmen, certain subjects provoke him, and awaken his fits of wrath. Marriage is one of these; in a hundred passages in his writings he rages against it; rages against children; an object of constant satire, even more contemptible in his eyes than a lord's chaplain, is a poor curate with a large family. The idea of this luckless paternity never fails to bring down from him gibes and foul language. Could [English writer Richard] Dick Steele, or [English writer Oliver] Goldsmith, or [English novelist Henry] Fielding, in his most reckless moment of satire, have written anything like the Dean's famous "modest proposal" for eating children [referring to Swift's famous satiric essay "A Modest Proposal"]? Not one of these but melts at the thoughts of childhood, fondles and caresses it. Mr. Dean has no such softness, and enters the nursery with the tread and gaiety of an ogre. "I have been assured," says he in the "Modest Proposal," "by a very knowing American of my acquaintance in London, that a young healthy child, well nursed, is, at a year old, a most delicious, nourishing, and wholesome food, whether stewed, roasted, baked, or boiled; and I make no doubt it will equally serve in a *ragoût.*" And taking up this pretty joke, as his way is, he argues it with perfect gravity and logic. He turns and twists this subject in a score of different ways: he hashes it; and he serves it up cold; and he garnishes it; and he relishes it always. He describes the little animal as "dropped from its dam," advising that the mother should let it suck plentifully in the last month, so as to render it plump and fat for a good table! "A child," says his Reverence, "will make two dishes at an entertainment for friends; and when the family dines alone, the fore or hind quarter will make a reasonable dish," and so on; and, the subject being so delightful that he can't leave it, he proceeds to recommend, in place of venison for squires' tables, "the bodies of young lads and maidens not exceeding fourteen or under twelve." Amiable humourist! laughing castigator of morals! There was a process well known and practised in the Dean's gay days: when a lout entered the coffee-house, the wags proceeded to what they called "roasting" him. This is roasting a subject with a vengeance. The Dean had a native genius for it. . . .

## SWIFT DESPISED MARRIAGE

And it was not merely by the sarcastic method that Swift exposed the unreasonableness of loving and having children. In Gulliver, the folly of love and marriage is urged by graver arguments and advice. In the famous Lilliputian kingdom, Swift speaks with approval of the practice of instantly removing children from their parents and educating them by the State; and amongst his favourite horses, a pair of foals are stated to be the very utmost a well-regulated equine couple would permit themselves. In fact, our great satirist was of opinion that conjugal love was unadvisable, and illustrated the theory by his own practice and example—God help him—which made him about the most wretched being in God's world.

## SWIFT'S LOGICAL ABSURDITY

The grave and logical conduct of an absurd proposition, as exemplified in the cannibal proposal just mentioned, is our author's constant method through all his works of humour. Given a country of people six inches or sixty feet high, and by the mere process of the logic, a thousand wonderful absurdities are evolved, at so many stages of the calculation. Turning to the first minister who waited behind him with a white staff near as tall as the mainmast of the "Royal Sovereign," the King of Brobdingnag observes how contemptible a thing human grandeur is, as represented by such a contemptible little creature as Gulliver. "The Emperor of Lilliput's features are strong and masculine" (what a surprising humour there is in this description!)—"The Emperor's features," Gulliver says, "are strong and masculine, with an Austrian lip, an arched nose, his, complexion olive, his countenance erect, his body and limbs well proportioned, and his deportment majestic. He is taller *by the breadth of my nail* than any of his court, which alone is enough to strike an awe into beholders."

## SWIFT'S HUMOUR AT ITS BEST

What a surprising humour there is in these descriptions! How noble the satire is here! how just and honest! How perfect the image! [British writer] Mr. [Thomas] Macaulay has quoted the charming lines of the poet, where the king of the pigmies is measured by the same standard. We have all read in [English poet John] Milton of the spear that was like "the mast of some tall admiral," but these images are surely likely to come to the comic poet originally. The subject is before him. He is turning it in a thousand ways. He is full of it. The figure suggests itself naturally to him, and comes out of his subject, as in that wonderful passage, when Gulliver's box having been dropped by the eagle into the sea, and Gulliver having been received into the ship's cabin, he calls upon the crew to bring the box into the cabin, and put it on the table, the cabin being only a quarter the size of the box. It is the *veracity* of the blunder which is so admirable. Had a man come from such a country as Brobdingnag he would have blundered so.

But the best stroke of humour, if there be a best in that abounding book, is that where Gulliver, in the unpronounceable country, describes his parting from his master the horse. "I took," he says, "a second leave of my master, but as I was going to prostrate myself to kiss his hoof, he did me the honour to raise it gently to my mouth. I am not ignorant how much I have been censured for mentioning this last particular. Detractors are pleased to think it improbable that so illustrious a person should descend to give so great a mark of distinction to a creature so inferior as I. Neither have I forgotten how apt some travellers are to boast of extraordinary favours they have received. But if these censurers were better acquainted with the noble and courteous disposition of the Houyhnhnms they would soon change their opinion."

The surprise here, the audacity of circumstantial evidence, the astounding gravity of the speaker, who is not ignorant how much he has been censured, the nature of the favour conferred, and the respectful exultation at the receipt of it, are surely complete; it is truth topsy-turvy, entirely logical and absurd.

## "Gulliver's Travels" Is Morally Shameful

As for the humour and conduct of this famous fable, I suppose there is no person who reads but must admire; as for the moral, I think it horrible, shameful, unmanly, blasphemous; and giant and great as this Dean is, I say we should hoot him. Some of this audience may n't have read the last part of Gulliver, and to such I would recall the advice of the venerable Mr. Punch to persons about to marry, and say "Don't." When Gulliver first lands among the Yahoos, the naked howling wretches clamber up trees and assault him, and he describes himself as "almost stifled with the filth which fell about him." The reader of the fourth part of "Gulliver's Travels" is like the hero himself in this instance. It is Yahoo language: a monster gibbering shrieks, and gnashing imprecations against mankind—tearing down all shreds of modesty, past all sense of manliness and shame; filthy in word, filthy in thought, furious, raging, obscene.

And dreadful it is to think that Swift knew the tendency of his creed—the fatal rocks towards which his logic desperately drifted. That last part of "Gulliver" is only a consequence of what has gone before; and the worthlessness of all mankind, the pettiness, cruelty, pride, imbecility, the general vanity, the foolish pretension, the mock greatness, the pompous dulness, the mean aims, the base successes—all these were present to him; it was with the din of these curses of the world, blasphemies against heaven, shrieking in his ears, that he began to write his dreadful allegory—of which the meaning is that man is utterly wicked, desperate, and imbecile, and his passions are so monstrous, and his boasted powers so mean, that he is and deserves to be the slave of brutes, and ignorance is better than his vaunted reason. What had this man done? what secret remorse was rankling at his heart? what fever was boiling in him, that he should see all the world blood-shot? We view the world with our own eyes, each of us; and we make from within us the world we see. A weary heart gets no gladness out of sunshine; a selfish man is sceptical about friendship, as a man with no ear doesn't care for music. A frightful self-consciousness it must have been, which looked on mankind so darkly through those keen eyes of Swift.

## THE MOST UNHAPPY MAN ON EARTH

A remarkable story is told by Scott, of [Swift's close friend Patrick] Delany, who interrupted Archbishop [of Dublin] King and Swift in a conversation which left the prelate in tears, and from which Swift rushed away with marks of strong terror and agitation in his countenance, upon which the Archbishop said to Delany, "You have just met the most unhappy man on earth; but on the subject of his wretchedness you must never ask a question."

The most unhappy man on earth;—Miserrimus [most wretched]—what a character of him! And at this time all the great wits of England had been at his feet. All Ireland had shouted after him, and worshipped him as a liberator, a saviour, the greatest Irish patriot and citizen. Dean Drapier Bickerstaff Gulliver [Swift's titles and nicknames]—the most famous statesmen, and the greatest poets of his day, had applauded him, and done him homage; and at this time, writing over to Bolingbroke from Ireland, he says, "It is time for me to have done with the world, and so I would if I could get into a better before I was called into the best, *and not die here in a rage, like a poisoned rat in a hole.*"

# Swift's Unhappy Utopia

George Orwell

As the creator of two of the most famous fictional societies of the twentieth century in his novels *Animal
Farm* and *Nineteen Eighty-Four*, George Orwell knows
well the process by which Swift conceived of far-off,
exotic worlds in *Gulliver's Travels*. Though Orwell
greatly admires *Gulliver's Travels* as a book written
with "the force of belief," he suggests that Swift, who
could find no joy in this world and who didn't appear
to believe in an afterlife, was unable to see the possibility of happiness. Thus Swift creates the world of the
Houyhnhnms, a society that is supposedly perfect, but
which turns out to be coldly rational and dull. Despite
his disagreement with Swift's pessimistic worldview,
Orwell acknowledges the uncomfortable truths contained in *Gulliver's Travels*. Orwell's essay, "Politics vs.
Literature: an Examination of *Gulliver's Travels*," from
which this selection is excerpted, appears in *Shooting
an Elephant and Other Essays*, a volume which contains such famous essays as "A Hanging," and "Politics
and the English Language."

We are right to think of Swift as a rebel and iconoclast, but
except in certain secondary matters, such as his insistence
that women should receive the same education as men, he
cannot be labelled "Left." He is a Tory [English Conservative
Party] anarchist, despising authority while disbelieving in
liberty, and preserving the aristocratic outlook while seeing
clearly that the existing aristocracy is degenerate and contemptible. When Swift utters one of his characteristic dia-
tribes [verbal attacks] against the rich and powerful, one
must probably, as I said earlier, write off something for the
fact that he himself belonged to the less successful party,
and was personally disappointed. The "outs," for obvious
reasons, are always more radical than the "ins." But the

most essential thing in Swift is his inability to believe that life—ordinary life on the solid earth, and not some rationalized, deodorized version of it—could be made worth living. Of course, no honest person claims that happiness is *now* a normal condition among adult human beings; but perhaps it *could* be made normal, and it is upon this question that all serious political controversy really turns. Swift has much in common—more, I believe, than has been noticed—with [Russian novelist Leo] Tolstoy, another disbeliever in the possibility of happiness. In both men you have the same anarchistic outlook covering an authoritarian cast of mind; in both a similar hostility to Science, the same impatience with opponents, the same inability to see the importance of any question not interesting to themselves; and in both cases a sort of horror of the actual process of life. . . . Tolstoy was a reformed rake who ended by preaching complete celibacy, while continuing to practise the opposite into extreme old age. Swift was presumably impotent, and had an exaggerated horror of human dung: he also thought about it incessantly, as is evident throughout his works. Such people are not likely to enjoy even the small amount of happiness that falls to most human beings and, from obvious motives, are not likely to admit that earthly life is capable of much improvement. Their incuriosity, and hence their intolerance, spring from the same root.

## THE HOUYHNHNMS' ARTIFICIAL PARADISE

Swift's disgust, rancor and pessimism would make sense against the background of a "next world" to which this one is the prelude. As he does not appear to believe seriously in any such thing, it becomes necessary to construct a paradise supposedly existing on the surface of the earth, but something quite different from anything we know, with all that he disapproves of—lies, folly, change, enthusiasm, pleasure, love and dirt—eliminated from it. As his ideal being he chooses the horse, an animal whose excrement is not offensive. The Houyhnhnms are dreary beasts—this is so generally admitted that the point is not worth laboring. Swift's genius can make them credible, but there can have been very few readers in whom they have excited any feeling beyond dislike. And this is not from wounded vanity at seeing animals preferred to men; for, of the two, the Houyhnhnms are much liker to human beings than are the Yahoos, and Gulliver's horror of the Yahoos, together with his recognition that they are the same kind of creature as himself, contains a logical absurdity. This horror comes upon him at his very first sight of them. "I never beheld," he says, "in all my Travels, so disagreeable an Animal, nor one against which I naturally conceived so strong an Antipathy." But in comparison with what are the Yahoos disgusting? Not with the Houyhnhnms, because at this time Gulliver has not seen a Houyhnhnm. It can only be in comparison with himself, i.e. with a human being. Later, however, we are to be told that the Yahoos *are* human beings, and human society becomes insupportable to Gulliver because all men are Yahoos. In that case why did he not conceive his disgust of humanity earlier? In effect we are told that the Yahoos are fantastically different from men, and yet are the same. Swift has over-reached himself in his fury, and is shouting at his fellow-creatures: "You are filthier than you are!" However, it is impossible to feel much sympathy with the Yahoos, and it is not because they oppress the Yahoos that the Houyhnhnms are unattractive. They are unattractive because the "Reason" by which they are governed is really a desire for death. They are exempt from love, friendship, curiosity, fear, sorrow and—except in their feelings towards the Yahoos, who occupy rather the same place in their community as the Jews in Nazi Germany—anger and hatred. "They have no Fondness for their Colts or Foles, but the Care they take, in educating them, proceeds entirely from the Dictates of *Reason.*" They lay store by "Friendship" and "Benevolence," but "these are not confined to particular Objects, but universal to the whole Race." They also value conversation, but in their conversations there are no differences of opinion, and "nothing passed but what was useful, expressed in the fewest and most significant Words." They practise strict birth control, each couple producing two offspring and thereafter abstaining from sexual intercourse. Their marriages are arranged for them by their elders, on eugenic principles, and their language contains no word for "love," in the sexual sense. When somebody dies they carry on exactly as before, without feeling any grief. It will be seen that their aim is to be as like a corpse as is possible while retaining physical life. One or two of their characteristics, it is true, do not seem to be strictly "reasonable" in their own usage of the word. Thus, they place a great value not only on physical hardihood but on athleticism, and they are devoted to poetry. But these exceptions may be less arbitrary than they seem. Swift probably emphasizes the physical strength of the Houyhnhnms in order to make clear that they could never be conquered by the hated human race, while a taste for poetry may figure among their qualities because poetry appeared to Swift as the antithesis of Science, from his point of view the most useless of all pursuits. In Part III he names "Imagination, Fancy, and Invention" as desirable faculties in which the Laputan mathematicians (in spite of their love of music) were wholly lacking. One must remember that although Swift was an admirable writer of comic verse, the kind of poetry he thought valuable would probably be didactic poetry. The poetry of the Houyhnhnms, he says—

> must be allowed to excel (that of) all other Mortals; wherein the Justness of their Similes, and the Minuteness, as well as exactness, of their Descriptions, are, indeed, inimitable. Their Verses abound very much in both of these; and usually contain either some exalted Notions of Friendship and Benevolence, or the Praises of those who were Victors in Races, and other bodily Exercises.

Alas, not even the genius of Swift was equal to producing a specimen by which we could judge the poetry of the Houyhnhnms. But it sounds as though it were chilly stuff (in heroic couplets, presumably), and not seriously in conflict with the principles of "Reason."

## A DREARY UTOPIA

Happiness is notoriously difficult to describe, and pictures of a just and well-ordered Society are seldom either attractive or convincing. Most creators of "favorable" Utopias, however, are concerned to show what life could be like if it were lived more fully. Swift advocates a simple refusal of life, justifying this by the claim that "Reason" consists in thwarting your instincts. The Houyhnhnms, creatures without a history, continue for generation after generation to live prudently, maintaining their population at exactly the same level, avoiding all passion, suffering from no diseases, meeting death indifferently, training up their young in the same principles—and all for what? In order that the same process may continue indefinitely. The notions that life here and now is worth living, or that it could be made worth living, or that it must be sacrificed for some future good, are all absent. The dreary world of the Houyhnhnms was about as good a Utopia as Swift could construct, granting that he neither believed in a "next world" nor could get any pleasure out of certain normal activities. But it is not really set up as something desirable in itself, but as the justification for another attack on humanity. The aim, as usual, is to humiliate Man by reminding him that he is weak and ridiculous, and above all that he stinks; and the ultimate motive, probably, is a kind of envy, the envy of the ghost for the living, of the man who knows he cannot be happy for the others who—so he fears—may be a little happier than himself. The political expression of such an outlook must be either reactionary [characterized by opposition to progress] or nihilistic [belief that all values are baseless], because the person who holds it will want to prevent Society from developing in some direction in which his pessimism may be cheated. One can do this either by blowing everything to pieces, or by averting social change. Swift ultimately blew everything to pieces in the only way that was feasible before the atomic bomb—that is, he went mad—but, as I have tried to show, his political aims were on the whole reactionary ones.

## ADMIRATION FOR SWIFT

From what I have written it may have seemed that I am *against* Swift, and that my object is to refute him and even to belittle him. In a political and moral sense I am against him, so far as I understand him. Yet curiously enough he is one of the writers I admire with least reserve, and *Gulliver's Travels*, in particular, is a book which it seems impossible for me to grow tired of. I read it first when I was eight—one day short of eight, to be exact, for I stole and furtively read the copy which was to be given me next day on my eighth birthday—and I have certainly not read it less than half a dozen times since. Its fascination seems inexhaustible. If I had to make a list of six books which were to be preserved when all others were destroyed, I would certainly put *Gulliver's Travels* among them. This raises the question: what is the relationship between agreement with a writer's opinions, and enjoyment of his work? . . .

## THE TRUTH IN SWIFT'S WRITING

If a book angers, wounds or alarms you, then you will not enjoy it, whatever its merits may be. If it seems to you a really pernicious book, likely to influence other people in some undesirable way, then you will probably construct an aesthetic theory to show that it *has* no merits. Current literary criticism consists quite largely of this kind of dodging to and fro between two sets of standards. And yet the opposite process can also happen: enjoyment can overwhelm disapproval, even though one clearly recognizes that one is enjoying something inimical. Swift, whose world-view is so peculiarly unacceptable, but who is nevertheless an extremely popular writer, is a good instance of this. Why is it that we don't mind being called Yahoos, although firmly convinced that we are *not* Yahoos?

It is not enough to make the usual answer that of course Swift was wrong, in fact he was insane, but he was "a good writer." It is true that the literary quality of a book is to some small extent separable from its subject-matter. Some people have a native gift for using words, as some people have a naturally "good eye" at games. It is largely a question of timing and of instinctively knowing how much emphasis to use. . . . But not all the power and simplicity of Swift's prose, nor the imaginative effort that has been able to make not one but a whole series of impossible worlds more credible than the majority of history books—none of this would enable us to enjoy Swift if his world-view were truly wounding or shocking. Millions of people, in many countries, must have enjoyed *Gulliver's Travels* while more or less seeing its anti-human implications: and even the child who accepts Parts I and II as a simple story gets a sense of absurdity from thinking of human beings six inches high. The explanation must be that Swift's world-view is felt to be *not* altogether false—or it would probably be more accurate to say, not false all the time. Swift is a diseased writer. He remains permanently in a depressed mood which in most people is only intermittent, rather as though someone suffering from jaundice or the after-effects of influenza should have the energy to write books. But we all know that mood, and something in us responds to the expression of it. . . . Swift falsifies his picture of the world by refusing to see anything in human life except dirt, folly and wickedness, but the part which he abstracts from the whole does exist, and it is something which we all know about while shrinking from mentioning it. Part of our minds—in any normal person it is the dominant part—believes that man is a noble animal and life is worth living: but there is also a sort of inner self which at least intermittently stands aghast at the horror of existence. In the queerest way, pleasure and disgust are linked together. The human body is beautiful: it is also repulsive and ridiculous, a fact which can be verified at any swimming pool. The sexual organs are objects of desire and also of loathing, so much so that in many languages, if not in all languages, their names are used as words of abuse. Meat is delicious, but a butcher's shop makes one feel sick: and indeed all our food springs ultimately from dung and dead bodies, the two things which of all others seem to us the most horrible. A child, when it is past the infantile stage but still looking at the world with fresh eyes, is moved by horror almost as often as by wonder—horror of snot and spittle, of the dogs' excrement on the pavement, the dying toad full of maggots, the sweaty smell of grown-ups, the hideousness of old men, with their bald heads and bulbous noses. In his endless harping on disease, dirt and deformity, Swift is not actually inventing anything, he is merely leaving something out. Human behavior, too, especially in politics, is as he describes it, although it contains other more important factors which he refuses to admit. So far as we can see, both horror and pain are necessary to the continuance of life on this planet, and it is therefore open to pessimists like Swift to say: "If horror and pain must always be with us, how can life be significantly improved?" His attitude is in effect the Christian attitude, minus the bribe of a "next world"—which, however, probably has less hold upon the minds of believers than the conviction that this world is a vale of tears and the grave is a place of rest. It is, I am certain, a wrong attitude, and one which could have harmful effects upon behavior; but something in us responds to it as it responds to the gloomy words of the burial service and the sweetish smell of corpses in a country church.

## THE FORCE OF BELIEF

It is often argued, at least by people who admit the importance of subject-matter, that a book cannot be "good" if it expresses a palpably false view of life. We are told that in our own age, for instance, any book that has genuine literary merit will also be more or less "progressive" in tendency. This ignores the fact that throughout history a similar struggle between progress and reaction has been raging, and that the best books of any one age have always been written from several different viewpoints, some of them palpably more false than others. In so far as a writer is a propagandist, the most one can ask of him is that he shall genuinely believe in what he is saying, and that it shall not be something blazingly silly. Today, for example, one can imagine a good book being written by a Catholic, a Communist, a Fascist, a pacifist, an anarchist, perhaps by an old-style Liberal or an ordinary Conservative: one cannot imagine a good book being written by a spiritualist [one who believes the dead communicate with the living], a Buchmanite [follower of evangelist Frank Buchman] or a member of the Ku Klux Klan. The views that a writer holds must be compatible with sanity, in the medical sense, and with the power of continuous thought: beyond that what we ask of him is talent, which is probably another name for conviction. Swift did not possess ordinary wisdom, but he did possess a terrible intensity of vision, capable of picking out a single hidden truth and then magnifying it and distorting it. The durability of *Gulliver's Travels* goes to show that, if the force of belief is behind it, a world-view which only just passes the test of sanity is sufficient to produce a great work of art.

# Reading *Gulliver's Travels* as a Child and as an Adult

Marcus Cunliffe

In his introduction to the Signet Edition of *Gulliver's Travels*, Marcus Cunliffe compares how children read Swift's classic to the way adults understand the book. Confronted in later years with an uncensored version of the classic, adults who have read *Gulliver* as children experience the book in a completely different way. The fanciful voyages to the lands of big and little people in which children delight become biting, satiric studies of human nature. Despite finding *Gulliver's Travels* to be an "inconsistent" masterpiece, Cunliffe defends both Swift and his book. The target of Swift's satire, human iniquity, is an "inexhaustible" one, but Swift's writing was up to the task. Marcus Cunliffe has taught at Manchester University. His many books include *Nation Takes Shape 1789–1837* and *In Search of America*.

It is in childhood, I suppose, that most of us are introduced to *Gulliver's Travels*—usually through an illustrated and slightly expurgated [censored] edition. We carry that childhood impression with us. We remember that the book is by Jonathan Swift, and perhaps that he was "Dean" Swift, a Church of England minister who was born and who died in Dublin. It is possible that the place and date of publication—London, 1726—stick with us. And we recall, more or less vividly, the events of the book itself: for instance, that Swift's imaginary traveller-narrator, Lemuel Gulliver, is a well-educated ship's surgeon who sails on four extraordinary voyages.

### *GULLIVER'S TRAVELS* SUMMARIZED

In the first of these Gulliver, shipwrecked, finds himself in *Lilliput*, whose alarmed inhabitants are only six inches high and so name him *Quinbus Flestrin*, the Man-Mountain. After many adventures, including eventual flight to the neighbouring kingdom of *Blefuscu*, Gulliver makes his way home to England. On a second voyage, he is by mischance left ashore in Brobdingnag, where the people are sixty feet tall and the Man-Mountain is therefore now a homunculus [a miniature human being], an amusing and vulnerable midget to them. His sojourn there ends when he is carried off by a Brobdingnagian eagle. It drops him (and the box in which he is housed) into the sea, and he is picked up by an English ship. The indefatigable Gulliver soon embarks on a third voyage. This time his experiences are more variegated. He visits the airborne island of *Laputa*, the home of a sort of absent-minded "power élite" who are absorbed in music, mathematics and abstract speculation. He wanders on to *Glubbdubdrib*, where the living can summon up the dead to act as their servants. Here Gulliver is thus able to talk with [Roman General Julius] Caesar and [Roman General Marcus] Brutus, [Greek epic poet] Homer and [Greek philosopher] Aristotle. Then he travels to *Luggnagg*, a land in which certain people known as *Struldbrugs* never die—though they do grow progressively older and more infirm. Once again he returns to England and to his patient family. Finally, on the fourth voyage Gulliver discovers a country ruled by handsome and highly rational horses, or *Houyhnhnms*. The human population consists of vicious, stupid, loathsome creatures called Yahoos in the Houyhnhnm language, and held in contempt and subjection by their Houyhnhnm masters. Gulliver himself is generously treated by the noble Houyhnhnms; yet they can regard him as at best only a superior form of Yahoo. To his distress they send him away. Reaching home at last, he realises that he has no home; for the rest of mankind, even his own family, appear to him as Yahoos whose presence he can hardly endure.

## READING *GULLIVER* AS A CHILD

Of these soberly depicted though intensely imagined episodes, the most memorable to children are no doubt the ones set in Lilliput and Brobdingnag. Here the visual ingenuity is richly pleasing, the ironical intent less evident. The topical allusions are unimportant: it does not matter to the young reader in the least that Swift was a Tory pamphleteer, desperately committed to the policies of his Tory patrons [fi-

## THE LEGACY OF *GULLIVER'S TRAVELS*

*Scholars refer to works that draw their inspiration from*
Gulliver's Travels *as Gulliveriana. In the eighteenth century
alone, at least sixty books of Gulliveriana were published. Several
involve trips to outer space and two even explore the moon. Gulliveriana has made a comeback in the twentieth century.*

Jonathan Swift's *Gulliver's Travels* was an immediate, widespread, and enduring success. Gulliveriana bear astonishingly
abundant tangible witness to that reception. Not every reader
has liked *Gulliver's Travels*, perhaps no one has put it first on
a list of favorite books, but an extraordinary number of people
have expressed their feelings about the book in imitative form.
This reaction began virtually the day Swift intimated that he
was writing a travel memoir. The phenomenon flourished for
about eighty years, lost momentum in the nineteenth century,
and has come alive again in our day.

New Gulliveriana are plentiful. For example, Swift's influence imbues Ryunosuke Akutagawa's 1927 pseudo-Utopian
satire on modern Japan, *Kappa*. In the name of Gulliver,
Matthew Hodgart wrote *A New Voyage to the Country of the
Houyhnhnms* after spending the summer of 1969 on an American college campus; his subtitle is "Wherein the Author returns and finds a New State of *Liberal Horses* and *Revolting
Yahoos*." Many a 1980s cartoon depicts a gigantic prostrate
Gulliver beset by a horde of tiny terrorists, health service or-
ganizations, bill collectors, or fruit flies. And there is a new
interest in the Gulliveriana produced by Swift's contemporaries and their immediate successors. Well over a hundred
eighteenth-century literary Gulliveriana are currently available in facsimile or modern editions. *Tom Thumb* among the
Gulliverian theatrical examples is never long off the boards,
in England or the United States. Early Gulliverian illustra-
tions, prints, drawings, and paintings have recently been reproduced, music reprinted and performed, and paintings fea-
tured in exhibitions. Certain Gulliveriana are successful
works in their own right. All provide information and insights
about Swift's book.

In two respects it is the Gulliveriana produced in the eighteenth century that are of paramount interest to the reader of
*Gulliver's Travels*. These make up the major share of Gulliveriana. More importantly, they are part of the original context
for Swift's book. Yet most readers today, even most eighteenth-
century specialists, have little awareness of them.

Jeanne K. Welcher, "Introduction" to *Gulliveriana VIII*. Delmar, NY: Scholar's
Facsimiles and Reprints, 1998, pp. 11–12.

nancial supports] Harley (the Earl of Oxford) and St. John (Viscount Bolingbroke), in whose downfall he shared; or, consequently, that Lilliput is a microcosm of British politics, with Blefuscu as France, the king as George I given over to treacherous Whig counsellors, and Gulliver perhaps as Bolingbroke; or that similar correspondences, to a smaller degree, may be traced throughout the narrative. What does count is the book's grave, circumstantial magic. Children are fascinated, after all, by *scale:* adults loom above them like Brobdingnagians, and the child's own dollhouse might be a home in Lilliput. Children are prepared to trust Gulliver as a reliable witness who does not indulge in whimsy or fantasy. So they can exult with him when he tows away the whole fleet of Blefuscu (though adult calculations suggest the task to be impossible), and share his dread when he is beset by rats as big as tigers, or sniffed at by elephantine cats and dogs. By contrast, the third and fourth voyages seem less actual. Children cannot see much relevance in Laputan eggheads, and may, if technologically inclined, doubt whether their "island" could really be kept aloft and propelled by a mere magnet; nor to them—as yet, at any rate—do people much resemble Yahoos.

## READING AS AN ADULT

Read the book again as an adult, especially in a reliable, unexpurgated [uncensored] edition, and you will emerge with a very different impression. Some of the charm may remain; yet the word "charm" will seem comically inadequate to define the strange and terrible intimations of *Gulliver's Travels.* Indeed to some adults, including such men of Swift's own century as Dr. Samuel Johnson, it is not so much a terrible as a horrible book, the product of a diseased and ultimately unhinged intellect, hateful because it is so full of hate for humankind. Consider the indictment that Swift puts into the mouth of the King of Brobdingnag, after Gulliver has described the governance of England:

> It doth not appear from all you have said, how any one virtue is required towards the procurement of any one station among you; much less that men are ennobled on account of their virtue, that priests are advanced for their piety or learning, soldiers for their conduct or valor, judges for their integrity, senators for the love of their country, or counsellors for their wisdom. As for yourself . . . who have spent the greatest part of your life in travelling, I am well disposed to hope

you may hitherto have escaped many vices of your country. But by what I have gathered from your own relation, and the answers I have with much pains wringed and extorted from you, I cannot but conclude the bulk of your natives to be the most pernicious race of little odious vermin that nature ever suffered to crawl upon the surface of the earth.

A dozen similar passages could be cited. Or consider the nausea that the human body apparently arouses in Gulliver, as when he sees the immense lice crawling on the beggars of Brobdingnag, or the naked flesh of maids of honor at the Brobdingnagian royal court:

Their skins appeared so coarse and uneven, so variously coloured when I saw them near, with a mole here and there as broad as a trencher, and hairs hanging from it thicker then packthreads; to say nothing further concerning the rest of their persons.

There are frequently references to diseases, bad smells, excrement. In an essay on Swift in *Do What You Will* (1929), Aldous Huxley contends that this was an obsessive preoccupation:

Swift hated bowels with such a passionate abhorrence that he felt a perverse compulsion to bathe continually in the squelchy imagination of them. Swift's greatness lies in the intensity, the almost insane violence of that "hatred of bowels" which is the essence of his misanthropy and which underlies the whole of his work.

Seen thus, Swift's writings could be "explained" as the nightmare vision of a misanthrope—a lonely, bitter person who never saw his father and was half-neglected by his mother: who never married, but instead exchanged gossip in baby-language with "Stella" (Esther Johnson): whose ambitions for preferment in the Church were thwarted: and who slumped into madness. Swift has been attacked on other grounds. In *Shooting an Elephant* (1950), George Orwell dismisses him as an evil-minded snob and reactionary who sneered at ordinary humanity and ridiculed intellectual effort.

Such are the extremes of distaste which Swift has aroused.

## COMING TO SWIFT'S DEFENCE

What can be said in his defence? A great deal, I think. In the first place, while certainly an unusual man, Swift was far from being a monster. He was *not* mentally unbalanced, though he did become senile toward the end of his long life, and though he did suffer from a complaint causing giddiness and vomiting which has since been diagnosed as labyrinthine vertigo, or Ménière's Syndrome. As for his alleged coarseness, this often reveals gusto rather than disgust; in his own day it was by no means exceptional, even among clerics. True, he probably never married. But celibacy is not a crime, and his relationship with "Stella" was idyllically close and harmonious. If he made enemies, he also developed lasting friendships; and he numbered among them [Alexander] Pope, [John] Arbuthnot, [John] Gay—some of the ablest and wittiest authors of his age, with whom he had much in common. True, he may have lost his chance of high clerical office (never rising beyond the semi-exile of the deanship of St. Patrick's, Dublin) through the irreverent tone of his writings. Nevertheless Swift was a sincere, even an old-fashioned Anglican, devout and conscientious: a third of his small income was regularly allotted to charity.

## In Defence of *Gulliver's Travels*

The man himself, then, is not particularly gross or grotesque. Nor is the lesson imparted by *Gulliver's Travels*. Not all mankind is portrayed as worthless and bestial. Swift has no fault to find, for example, with the Portuguese sea captain whom Gulliver meets after leaving the Yahoos. Swift may be an ironist but he is not a cynic: he cares too deeply. Gulliver inevitably reminds us of Candide [a satire by French writer Voltaire]; but Swift's narrative lacks the light, sustained, merciless Voltaireian hilarity. A letter written to Pope in 1725 affords a clue:

> I tell you after all, that I do not hate mankind: it is *vous autres* who hate them, because you would have them reasonable animals, and are angry for being disappointed.

In part, that is, Swift exhibits an orthodox Christian's disdain for Deism—for the facile, visionary optimism of those who believe that men are rational, and that reason provides them with an infallible system of right conduct. Hence his derisive treatment of the Laputans and the whole breed of "projectors" who try to impose their elaborate theories upon mankind. Some critics insist, too, that Swift means to imply that, while the Houyhnhnms are to be admired for their graceful rationality, their experience is of no real validity for human beings.

Men are fallible: they have also made things steadily worse for themselves. In other words, Swift assumes that in a former, yeoman order men had the dignity of simplicity.

This has been spoiled by kings and tyrants, courts, pride, wealth. To the curse of original sin has been added the subordinate curse of sophistication.

## AN INCONSISTENT MASTERPIECE

Are these arguments convincing? Not entirely, to me. I have no question that *Gulliver's Travels* is a magnificent, tremendous book. But it is not an altogether consistent book—a fault it shares with several other masterpieces. It says different things in varying voices. It is a work written over a period of several years; it is by turns extravaganza and diatribe, burlesque and sermon, squib and satire. One can understand why it irritated Orwell, though he himself was not always utterly consistent. Perhaps it mirrors the inconsistencies in Swift's own make-up—Swift the ribald minister; the Tory journalist who is yet a passionate believer in the Whig Revolution of 1688 and its attendant principles of freedom, decency, right-dealing; Swift the upholder of the Protestant Establishment in Ireland, who yet won a merited reputation as the Irish Patriot for his onslaught on English injustices; Swift the scurrilous and radical man of letters, who yet cherishes a nostalgic dream of an Old England where everyone knew his place and no place could be bought; Swift the intellectual who is scornful of the Laputan intellect, yet surely has no fault to find with the rationality practised by the Houyhnhnms (if only in order to sharpen the contrast with the stupid Yahoos); Swift who is endlessly aghast at the vice and folly of his fellow creatures, sickened and saddened, yet never bored, never at a loss for something to laugh and shudder at. He finished *Gulliver's Travels* in his fifty-eighth year, protesting in effect that he had lost his joy and his illusions, yet still ready to document the process with the fierce relish of a true-born Englishman. What a subject he has in that inexhaustible iniquity, what a weapon in that broadside irony.

# CHRONOLOGY

**1660**

Restoration of King Charles II; Royal Society is founded.

**1664**

Jonathan Swift Sr. marries Abigail Erick.

**1667**

Jonathan Swift is born on November 30.

**1669**

Swift is abducted by his nurse and taken to England.

**1673**

Enters Kilkenny Grammar School.

**1682**

Enters Trinity College in Dublin, Ireland.

**1686**

Receives bachelor's degree from Trinity.

**1688**

Glorious Revolution; Swift leaves Ireland due to "the Troubles."

**1689**

Enters service of Sir William Temple in England; accession to English throne of William III and Mary II; meets Esther "Stella" Johnson.

**1690**

Returns to Ireland.

**1691**

Resumes service with William Temple at Moor Park, England; publishes his first work, "Ode to the Athenian Society."

**1692**

Receives master's degree from Oxford.

**1694**

Returns to Ireland; is ordained as a deacon.

**1695**

Swift is ordained as a priest and is appointed to serve in Kilroot, near Belfast, Ireland.

**1696**

Returns to work for Temple in Moor Park.

**1699**

Serves as chaplain to Lord Berkeley in Dublin; Gulliver's first voyage.

**1700**

Becomes vicar of Laracor in Ireland.

**1701**

Receives doctor of divinity degree from the University of Dublin.

**1702**

Death of William III; Queen Anne ascends the English throne.

**1704**

Swift publishes *A Tale of a Tub* and *The Battle of the Books.*

**1707**

Swift is sent to England as emissary of the Church of Ireland.

**1708**

Publishes *The Bickerstaff Papers* and several poems.

**1709**

Returns to Ireland as Whig government is defeated by Tories.

**1710**

Swift is sent back to England; writes *The Examiner*, a Tory paper; meets Hester "Vanessa" Vanhomrigh.

**1711**

Writes numerous poems and pamphlets in support of Tory causes; begins composing letters that will be collected as his *Journal to Stella.*

**1713**

Swift is appointed dean of St. Patrick's Cathedral in Dublin.

**1714**

Returns to Ireland after the death of Queen Anne and the fall of the Tory government; publishes *The Public Spirit of the Whigs.*

**1715**

Gulliver's final return home.

**1720**

Publishes *A Proposal for the Universal Use of Irish Manufacture;* begins writing *Gulliver's Travels.*

**1723**

Tours southern and western Ireland; death of Hester Vanhomrigh.

**1724**

Writes and publishes *The Drapier's Letters,* a series of articles attacking the English for their exploitation of Ireland.

**1725**

Celebrated as an Irish patriot for opposing the Wood's halfpence scheme.

**1726**

*Gulliver's Travels* and "Cadenus and Vanessa" are published; famine in Ireland.

**1727**

Visits England for the last time; death of George I; George II ascends the throne of England.

**1728**

Death of Esther Johnson.

**1729**

Swift publishes "A Modest Proposal."

**1731**

Swift writes numerous poems, including "Verses on the Death of Dr. Swift."

**1740–1741**

Famine in Ireland.

**1742**

Swift's health fails rapidly; he is declared insane by a Commission of Lunacy.

**1745**

Jonathan Swift dies.

# FOR FURTHER RESEARCH

### ABOUT JONATHAN SWIFT

Keith Crook, *A Preface to Swift*. London: Longman, 1998.

J.A. Downie, *Jonathan Swift: Political Writer*. London: Routledge and Kegan Paul, 1984.

Irvin Ehrenpreis, *The Personality of Jonathan Swift*. Cambridge, MA: Harvard University Press, 1958.

———, *Swift: The Man, His Works, and the Age*. 3 vols. Cambridge, MA: Harvard University Press, 1962.

Victoria Glendinning, *Jonathan Swift*. London: Hutchinson, 1998.

David Nokes, *Jonathan Swift: A Hypocrite Reversed*. London: Oxford University Press, 1985.

### ABOUT *GULLIVER'S TRAVELS*

Liz Bellamy, *Jonathan Swift's* Gulliver's Travels. New York: St. Martin's, 1992.

Harold Bloom, *Jonathan Swift's* Gulliver's Travels. New York: Chelsea House, 1996.

Frank Brady, *Twentieth Century Interpretations of* Gulliver's Travels: *A Collection of Critical Essays*. Englewood Cliffs, NJ: Prentice-Hall, 1968.

Herbert Davis, *The Satire of Jonathan Swift*. New York: Macmillan, 1947.

Milton P. Foster, *A Casebook on Gulliver Among the Houyhnhnms*. New York: Cromwell, 1961.

Christopher Fox, ed., *Jonathan Swift:* Gulliver's Travels: *A Case Study in Contemporary Criticism*. New York: St. Martin's, 1995.

Richard Gravil, ed., *Swift: "Gulliver's Travels."* London: Macmillan, 1974.

Robert A. Greenberg, ed., Gulliver's Travels: *An Authoritative Text, the Correspondence of Swift, Pope's Verses on Gulliver's Travels, and Critical Essays*. New York: Norton, 1980.

Charles H. Hinnant, *Purity and Defilement in* Gulliver's Travels. New York: St. Martin's, 1987.

A. Norman Jeffares, ed., *Fair Liberty Was All His Cry: A Tercentenary Tribute to Jonathan Swift, 1667–1745.* London: Macmillan, 1967.

Ronald Knowles, Gulliver's Travels: *The Politics of Satire.* New York: Twayne, 1996.

Roger McHugh and Philip Edwards, *Jonathan Swift, 1667–1967: A Dublin Tercentenary Tribute.* London: Oxford University Press, 1967.

Ricardo Quintana, *Mind and Art of Jonathan Swift.* London: Oxford University Press, 1936.

———, *Swift: An Introduction.* London: Oxford University Press, 1955.

Claude Rawson, *The Character of Swift's Satire: A Revised Focus.* Newark: University of Delaware Press, 1983.

———, *Gulliver and the Gentle Reader: Studies in Swift and Our Time.* London: Routledge and Kegan Paul, 1973.

Edward J. Rielly, ed., *Approaches to Teaching* Gulliver's Travels. New York: Modern Language Association of America, 1988.

Frederick N. Smith, ed., *The Genres of* Gulliver's Travels. Newark: University of Delaware Press, 1990.

Ernest Tuveson, ed., *Swift: A Collection of Critical Essays.* Englewood Cliffs, NJ: Prentice-Hall, 1964.

Brian Vickers, ed., *The World of Jonathan Swift.* Oxford, England: Blackwell, 1968.

## ABOUT SEVENTEENTH- AND EIGHTEENTH-CENTURY BRITISH POLITICS AND HISTORY

Oliver W. Ferguson, *Jonathan Swift and Ireland.* Urbana: University of Illinois Press, 1962.

Geoffrey Holmes, ed., *Britain After the Glorious Revolution: 1689–1714.* London: Macmillan, 1969.

Louis A. Landa, *Swift and the Church of Ireland.* London: Oxford University Press, 1959.

David Ogg, *England in the Reign of Charles II.* London: Oxford University Press, 1963.

W.A. Speck, *Tory and Whig: The Struggle in the Constituencies, 1701–1715.* London: Macmillan, 1970.

# INDEX

Addison, Joseph, 22, 23
Age of Enlightenment, 55
Age of Reason, 53, 55
allegory, 78–79, 98–99, 102–103,
    120
anarchism, 80, 167
Anglican Church
    and Swift, 16, 18–22, 24-25,
    179–80
*Apology for Raymond de
    Sebonde* (Montaigne), 88
Arbuthnot, John
    friendship with Swift, 22, 24,
    58, 179
    on *Gulliver's Travels*, 28, 62–64
Asimov, Isaac
    on Swift, 12
Auden, W.H., 45

Balnibarbi (island), 36, 60
*Battle of the Books, The*, 19, 21
Beckett, Samuel, 45, 47
Bergerac, Cyrano de, 70
Berkeley, George, 125, 135
Bickerstaff, Isaac, 22, 27, 165
Blefescu
    as France, 78, 177
    Gulliver defeats, 33–34, 118
    location of, 59
Boswell, James, 134, 157
*Brave New World* (Huxley), 44,
    46, 48
Brobdingnag
    compared to England, 78,
    129–31, 137–38

compared to Lilliput, 126–32,
    134
king of
    conversations with
    Gulliver, 35, 128–31, 138
    description of, 31–32, 132
    on the English, 35, 130–32,
    137, 177–78
    language in, 83, 85, 86
    location of, 59–60
    as political utopia, 78, 139
    sizes in, 71, 103–104
    metaphor for morality,
    123–33, 134–40
Bullitt, John M., 100
Bunyan, John, 64, 67
Burke, Edmund, 61
Byron, Lord (George), 47

Cabell, James, 46
"Cadenus and Vanessa," 25
Campbell, Roy, 45
*Candide* (Voltaire), 44, 46, 179
Cervantes, Miguel de, 48
characters
    emperor of Lilliput
    description of, 31, 101–102,
    119, 132, 162
    treatment of Gulliver, 117,
    118, 121
Flimnap, 31, 103
Glumdalclitch, 31, 125–26,
    127, 158
Gulliver
    as allegory, 120

as Bolingbroke, 78, 177
change in, 119, 123, 126,
  131–32
compared to Yahoos, 148
description of, 31
innocence of, 119, 131
as mechanical toy, 103–104
mental trials of, 92
morality of, 116–21, 126
narrative style, 96, 97
physical trials of, 91–95,
  126–27
psychological action, 126
reader identifies with,
  131–32
speaks to famous dead, 37,
  143–44
as Swift, 147, 165
as unreliable narrator, 83,
  89–90, 96–99, 105
as a writer, 88–90
Houyhnhnms
compared to humans, 167,
  179
compared to Laputans,
  145–46
description of, 31, 99, 168
language of, 84–85, 86
limitations of, 145–46,
  147–53, 167–69
and reason, 53, 79, 145–46,
  147–48, 150–51, 168, 179
king of Brobdingnag
conversations with Gulliver,
  35, 128–31, 138
description of, 31–32, 132
on the English, 35, 130–32,
  137, 177–78
Lilliputians
characters of, 77, 120–22
mechanical symbolism, 101
Lord Munodi, 32, 110
Pedro de Mendez, 32
Projectors
Gulliver as, 146
satire of Royal Society, 79, 99,
  110–14, 179
Reldresal, 32, 121

Skyresh Bolgolam, 32, 121
Struldbruggs, 32, 37, 144–45
Yahoos
allegory, 164
compared to Gulliver, 148
compared to human beings,
  149–50, 164, 167–68, 171
description of, 32
Swift on, 60–61
Chesterton, Gilbert, 45
Christian humanism, 53
Churchill, Charles, 45
"Conduct of the Allies, The," 23,
  76
Cunliffe, Marcus, 174

Dampier, William, 26, 58–60,
  89, 106, 124
Defoe, Daniel
compared to Swift, 66–75, 80
and *Robinson Crusoe*, 26, 60,
  107–108
Dennis, Nigel, 65
DePorte, Michael, 141
Derham, William, 111
Descartes, René, 54
Dingley, Rebecca, 21, 24–25
*Discovery of a New World* (Hall),
  70
*Dissensions in Athens and
  Rome*, 21
Donoghue, Denis, 150–51
*Don Quixote* (Cervantes), 48, 60
Douglas, Norman, 45
*Drapier's Letters, The*, 26, 76, 77,
  79, 160
Dryden, John, 13, 18, 44, 45, 52

Ehrenpreis, Irwin, 30
Eliot, T.S., 13
Erskine-Hill, Howard, 123
*Examiner, The*, 22–23

Feinberg, Leonard, 41
Ford, Boris, 147
Ford, Charles, 26, 27, 60
France, Anatole, 44, 46
Fussell, Paul, 91

*Gargantua and Pantagruel*
(Rabelais), 70
Gay, John
friendship with Swift, 23–24,
28, 58, 179
on reactions to *Gulliver's
Travels,* 27, 64
Genet, Jean, 45
Gilbert, Jack C., 116
Glendinning, Victoria
on Swift, 19–20, 22, 24
Glubdubdrib
dead in, 37, 143–44
language in, 85
Godwin, William, 80
Great Britain
history of, 15–17, 22–23,
25–26, 52–56
satire of, 16, 23, 76–80, 130–32,
136–40, 143
*Gulliver's Travels*
adult reading of, 177–80
bodily functions in, 68–69,
70–73, 112, 120, 127–28, 135,
178
censored, 27–28, 62, 77, 135,
174
and children
reading of, 41, 135, 170, 171,
174–75, 177
stories for, 57–58
compared to *A Tale of a Tub,*
56, 57, 73, 105
compared to *Robinson
Crusoe,* 65–75, 125
parody of, 105–109
ending of, 38–39, 74–75, 108
failure of language in, 82–90
genesis of, 24, 26, 58–59
grounded in reality, 70–73
Gulliveriana, 176
parodies first-person
memoirs, 105–109
Part I
comparing Lilliput to
Europe, 134–40
mechanical symbolism in,
101–104

satire
political, 77, 119, 121–22,
177
religious, 102–103, 122
summary, 32–34
Part II
comparing Brobdingnag to
Europe, 134–40
mechanical symbolism in,
101, 103–104
political satire, 77, 128–31,
137–40
summary, 34–35
Part III
satire
political, 77, 143
on wishful thinking, 142
summary, 36–37
Part IV
political satire, 77
summary, 37–39
political allegory in, 77–79,
102–103, 119, 121
precursors to, 70–71
responses to
belief, 28, 63, 170–72
brilliant satire, 155–59
disbelief, 28, 63, 106, 171–72
morally shameful, 163–64
popularity of, 27, 62–63, 135
product of sick mind,
160–65, 166–73, 177
satire
on English history, 16, 23
on humanity, 27, 57–58,
149–50, 164, 167–68, 171
of religion, 19, 63, 77–78,
102–103, 122
self-referential book, 88–89
style of, 58–59
suppression of, 27–28, 62, 78
writing of, 26, 60, 145

Hall, Joseph, 70
Halley, Edmund, 110, 111
Harley, Robert (Lord Oxford)
friendship with Swift, 22, 24,
36, 58, 66, 177

as Gulliver, 78, 119, 120
patron of Swift, 22, 36, 66, 177
Hazlitt, William, 155
Heine, Heinrich, 43
*History of the Royal Society of
London* (Sprat), 111
Hobbes, Thomas, 54, 120
Hodgart, Matthew, 76, 176
Hooke, Robert, 111
Hunter, J. Paul, 105
Huxley, Aldous, 44, 46, 48, 178

*Isle of Pines* (Neville), 70

Johnson, Esther (Stella)
death, 27, 28
description of, 20
friendship with Swift, 17,
19–21, 24, 25, 60, 79, 179
Swift's letters to, 24, 79
Johnson, Samuel
dislike of Swift, 62, 134, 156,
157, 177
satire by, 45, 46
writings of, 95, 114, 156
*Journal to Stella, The,* 24
Joyce, James, 45
*Jurgen* (Cabell), 44, 46
Juvenal, 42, 44, 47, 95

Lagado
language in, 111–12
satire of science, 110–14,
142–43, 179
writing in, 86–87, 112
Landa, Louis A., 29
language
failure in *Gulliver's Travels,*
82–90
lying, 85–86
nautical, 83, 123–24
scientific, 83, 85, 111–12
truth telling, 85
Laputa
allegory of England, 77–79
compared to Houyhnhnms,
145–46
language in, 83

location of, 36, 60
pun on utopia, 143
world without hope, 141, 144
Lawrence, Karen, 96
Lecky, W.E.H., 14
*Leviathan* (Hobbes), 54
Lewis, Sinclair, 44, 48, 49
Lilliput
compared to Brobdingnag,
126–32, 134
emperor of
description of, 31, 101–102,
119, 132, 162
treatment of Gulliver, 117,
118, 121
language of, 83, 85
Lilliputians
characters of, 77, 120–22
mechanical symbolism, 101
location of, 59
sizes in, 71–72, 101–104
metaphor for morality,
116–22, 134–40
utopian aspects, 77, 137, 139
Lindalino
as political allegory, 78–79
Locke, John, 55
Lucian, 70
Luggnagg
land of Struldbruggs, 37,
144–45
location of, 60

Machiavelli, 45, 46
Mandeville, Bernard, 45
*Mandragola* (Machiavelli), 46
Marvell, Andrew, 45
*Mechanical Operation of the
Spirit, The,* 21, 101
Mencken, H.L., 45–49
metaphor
clothing as, 93–94
sizes
in Brobdingnag, 123–33,
134–40
in Lilliput, 116–22, 134–40
Mezciems, Jenny, 143
*Micrographia or Some*

*Physiological Description of Minute Bodies Made by Magnifying Glasses* (Hooke), 111
"Modest Proposal, A"
　cannibalism in, 48, 66–67, 161
　satire of, 12, 44, 66–67
　style of, 89, 99
Monk, Samuel H., 98
Montaigne, Michel de, 88
More, Sir Thomas, 70, 130, 144
Motte, Benjamin, 27
Musset, Alfred de, 43

Neville, Henry, 70
Newton, Isaac, 54, 79, 110, 111
*New Voyage to the Country of the Houyhnhnms, A,* (Hodgart), 76, 176
Nokes, David, 15, 22
Novak, Maximillian E., 71

"Ode to the Athenian Society," 17
Orwell, George, 166, 178, 180

Parnell, Thomas, 24, 58
*Penguin Island* (France), 46
Pinkus, Philip, 51
Pirandello, Luigi, 45
political parties. *See* Tories; Whigs
Pope, Alexander
　friendship with Swift, 23–24, 58, 59, 61, 179
　on *Gulliver's Travels,* 64, 73
　satire, 47, 87
　on science, 54, 114
　Scriblerus Club, 23–24, 58
　writings of, 23, 87
"Predictions for the Year 1708," 22
*Principia* (Newton), 111
*Principles of Philosophy* (Descartes), 54
Probyn, Clive T., 110
*Proposal for the Universal Use of Irish Manufactures, A,* 25–26

Rabelais, Francois, 44, 47, 70, 128
rationalism, 55
Ratner, Lois, 96
religion
　and political parties, 23, 24, 52–53
　satire on, 19, 63, 77–78, 102–103, 122
　in scientific age, 54–56
　themes, 95, 121
*Robinson Crusoe* (Defoe), 26, 60, 71
　as documentary, 69
　compared to *Gulliver's Travels,* 65-75, 125
　parodied in, 105–109
　ending of, 74–75
　and materialism, 67–69, 73–74
Rogers, Woodes, 71
Rowse, A.L., 14, 57
Royal Society
　formation of, 54
　and Gulliver, 89, 91
　satire of, 79, 87, 99, 110–14, 179

satire
　age of, 51–52
　and Alexander Pope, 47, 87
　in "A Modest Proposal," 12, 44, 66–67
　definition of, 41–42, 50
　didactic, 45
　on Great Britain, 16, 23, 76–80, 130–32, 136–40, 143
　Horatian, 42, 44
　humanist, 45
　on humanity, 27, 57–58, 149–50, 164, 167–68, 171
　and inconsistency, 143
　Juvenalian, 42, 44
　on language, 82–90, 97, 111
　Marxist, 45
　moral, 136

must be relevant, 44–45
and originality, 48
pleasures of, 43–44
of politics, 76–80, 119, 121–22,
   128–31, 136–40, 143
purposes of, 48–50
and reason, 42–43
reducing men to machines,
   100–104
of religion, 19, 63, 77–78,
   102–103, 122
and Samuel Johnson, 45, 46
on science, 79, 99, 110–14,
   142–43, 146, 179
and social norms, 45–46
Thomist, 45
unfairness of, 46–47
use of distortion, 42
on wishful thinking, 142
Schopenhauer, Arthur, 42
science
   age of, 53–54, 110–11
   Alexander Pope on, 54, 114
   language of, 83, 85, 111–12
   and religion, 54–56
   satire of, 79, 110–14, 142–43,
      146, 179
   Swift on, 79, 87, 110–14, 167,
      169
Scriblerus Club, 24, 26, 58
Seifter, Betsy, 96
Selkirk, Alexander, 26, 60, 71,
   109
sentimentalism, 55
Shaw, Bernard, 44, 45, 49
*Shortest Way with the Dissenters,
   The*, (Defoe), 66
Speck, W.A., 134
Sprat, Bishop, 111–12
St. John, Henry (Viscount
   Bolingbroke)
   as character in *Gulliver's
      Travels*, 36, 78, 110, 119–20
   disapproval of *Gulliver's
      Travels*, 63
   friendship with Swift, 22, 28,
      60, 165
   patron of Swift, 22, 177

Steele, Richard, 22, 23
Swift, Abigail (mother), 13–14
Swift, Godwin (uncle), 13–15
Swift, Jonathan
   autobiography of, 13–14, 20,
      21, 28–30, 155, 165
   birth of, 13
   careers of, 12
      in Anglican Church, 16,
         18–22, 24–25, 179–80
   on children, 161–62
   compared to Defoe, 66–75, 80
   compared to Tolstoy, 167
   death of, 30
   defense of, 155–59, 178–79
   education of, 13–15, 18, 21
   experiment in optics, 134–40
   as Gulliver, 147, 165
   on *Gulliver's Travels*, 26, 27,
      60, 77
   illness of
      mental, 29–30, 170–71, 178
      physical, 17, 26, 28, 29, 60,
         178–79
   inconsistencies in, 179–80
   influence of, on other writers,
      176
   and Irish politics, 25, 26, 76
   letters of, 24, 59, 61, 79, 179
   literary reputation of, 12–13
   on marriage, 161–62
   misanthropic views, 57–59,
      61–62, 147, 152, 160–64,
      166–71, 178
   misunderstood, 155–59
   moral self-knowledge, 114
   opinions on science, 79, 87,
      110–14, 167, 169
   patrons of, 18, 24, 36, 58, 177
   poetry of, 17–18, 28–30, 52,
      169
   political activity, 16–17, 21–25,
      66–67, 76, 129, 166, 175
   political allegory, 77–78,
      102–103
   satire
      of English politics, 76–80,
         138–40, 143, 177

enhanced by technique,
    100-104
of religion, 19, 63, 77-78, 102
of writing, 82, 85, 86-88, 97
Scriblerus Club, 24, 26, 58
and Sir William Temple, 13,
    16-20, 69
time period of, 51-56
travels of, 12
writing anonymously, 19,
    21-22, 26, 27-28, 57, 62, 165
writing career, 15, 17-23
on Yahoos, 60-61
symbolism, 101-104

*Tale of a Tub, A*
attack on Hobbes's theories, 54
compared to *Gulliver's Travels*,
    56, 57, 73, 89, 94, 105, 157
excellence of, 19, 156
as ironic satire, 15, 19, 89, 94,
    155
publishing of, 19, 21
Temple, Sir William
influence on Swift, 13, 16-19,
    69
as king of Brobdingnag, 78
as Lord Munodi, 110
Swift as literary executor, 20
Swift works for, 17-20
Thackeray, William Makepeace,
    160
themes
books, 85, 87-88, 94-95
human frailties, 91-95
religious, 95, 121
war, 80, 119, 131-32
Tippett, Brian, 82
Tolstoy, Leo, 167
Tories
in Brobdingnag, 78
description of, 17, 52

fall from power, 23-24
in *Gulliver's Travels*, 78, 129,
    131-32
Swift becomes, 22-23, 166
*True Story* (Lucian), 70

utopia
Brobdingnag as, 78, 139
false hopes of, 143, 144, 145
and Houyhnhnms, 169-70
and Laputa, 143
Lilliput as, 77, 137, 139
*Utopia* (More), 70, 130

Vanhomrigh, Hesther (Vanessa),
    24, 25, 68
"Verses on the Death of Dr.
    Swift," 28-30, 155
Voltaire, 44, 46, 47
*Voyages* (Dampier), 26, 58, 124

Welcher, Jeanne K., 176
Whigs
description of, 23, 52
in *Gulliver's Travels*, 27, 58,
    129, 131-32
in power, 17, 23-24
Swift as, 17, 22
Whiteway, Martha, 29
Wilde, Oscar, 42, 45
Wycherley, William, 45

Yahoos
allegory, 164
compared to Gulliver, 148
compared to human beings,
    149-50, 164, 167-68, 171
description of, 32
Swift on, 60-61
Yeats, William Butler, 13, 30

Zimmerman, Everett, 89